SEAMUS HEANEY

Modern Critical Views

Henry Adams
Edward Albee
A. R. Ammons
Matthew Arnold
John Ashbery
W. H. Auden
Jane Austen
James Baldwin
Charles Baudelaire
Samuel Beckett
Saul Bellow
The Bible
Elizabeth Bishop
William Blake
Jorge Luis Borges
Elizabeth Bowen
Bertolt Brecht
The Brontës
Robert Browning
Anthony Burgess
George Gordon, Lord
   Byron
Thomas Carlyle
Lewis Carroll
Willa Cather
Cervantes
Geoffrey Chaucer
Kate Chopin
Samuel Taylor Coleridge
Joseph Conrad
Contemporary Poets
Hart Crane
Stephen Crane
Dante
Charles Dickens
Emily Dickinson
John Donne & The
   Seventeenth-Century
   Metaphysical Poets
Elizabethan Dramatists
Theodore Dreiser
John Dryden
George Eliot
T. S. Eliot
Ralph Ellison
Ralph Waldo Emerson
William Faulkner
Henry Fielding
F. Scott Fitzgerald
Gustave Flaubert
E. M. Forster
Sigmund Freud
Robert Frost

Robert Graves
Graham Greene
Thomas Hardy
Nathaniel Hawthorne
William Hazlitt
Seamus Heaney
Ernest Hemingway
Geoffrey Hill
Friedrich Hölderlin
Homer
Gerard Manley Hopkins
William Dean Howells
Zora Neale Hurston
Henry James
Samuel Johnson and
   James Boswell
Ben Jonson
James Joyce
Franz Kafka
John Keats
Rudyard Kipling
D. H. Lawrence
John Le Carré
Ursula K. Le Guin
Doris Lessing
Sinclair Lewis
Robert Lowell
Norman Mailer
Bernard Malamud
Thomas Mann
Christopher Marlowe
Carson McCullers
Herman Melville
James Merrill
Arthur Miller
John Milton
Eugenio Montale
Marianne Moore
Iris Murdoch
Vladimir Nabokov
Joyce Carol Oates
Sean O'Casey
Flannery O'Connor
Eugene O'Neill
George Orwell
Cynthia Ozick
Walter Pater
Walker Percy
Harold Pinter
Plato
Edgar Allan Poe

Poets of Sensibility & the
   Sublime
Alexander Pope
Katherine Anne Porter
Ezra Pound
Pre-Raphaelite Poets
Marcel Proust
Thomas Pynchon
Arthur Rimbaud
Theodore Roethke
Philip Roth
John Ruskin
J. D. Salinger
Gershom Scholem
William Shakespeare
   (3 vols.)
   Histories & Poems
   Comedies
   Tragedies
George Bernard Shaw
Mary Wollstonecraft
   Shelley
Percy Bysshe Shelley
Edmund Spenser
Gertrude Stein
John Steinbeck
Laurence Sterne
Wallace Stevens
Tom Stoppard
Jonathan Swift
Alfred, Lord Tennyson
William Makepeace
   Thackeray
Henry David Thoreau
Leo Tolstoi
Anthony Trollope
Mark Twain
John Updike
Gore Vidal
Virgil
Robert Penn Warren
Evelyn Waugh
Eudora Welty
Nathanael West
Edith Wharton
Walt Whitman
Oscar Wilde
Tennessee Williams
William Carlos Williams
Thomas Wolfe
Virginia Woolf
William Wordsworth
Richard Wright
William Butler Yeats

These and other titles in preparation

Modern Critical Views

SEAMUS HEANEY

Edited and with an introduction by
Harold Bloom
Sterling Professor of the Humanities
Yale University

CHELSEA HOUSE PUBLISHERS ◊ 1986
New Haven ◊ New York ◊ Philadelphia

© 1986 by Chelsea House Publishers, a division of Chelsea House
Educational Communications, Inc.

133 Christopher Street, New York, NY 10014
345 Whitney Avenue, New Haven, CT 06511
5014 West Chester Pike, Edgemont, PA 19028

Printed and bound in the United States of America

The paper used in this publication meets the minimum
requirements of the American National Standard for Permanence of
Paper for Printed Library Materials, Z39.48-1984.

Library of Congress Cataloging-in-Publication Data
Main entry under title:

Seamus Heaney.

(Modern critical views)
Bibliography: p.
Includes index.
1. Heaney, Seamus—Criticism and interpretation—
Addresses, essays, lectures. I. Bloom, Harold.
II. Series.
PR6058. E2Z87 1986   821'.914   85–27995
ISBN 0–87754–702–5

Contents

Editor's Note

This volume gathers together a representative selection of the best criticism so far devoted to the work of the Northern Irish poet Seamus Heaney. Except for the editor's introduction, originally published as an overview of Heaney's first five books (through *Field Work*), it is arranged in the chronological order of publication of these essays. The editor acknowledges with gratitude the assistance of his researchers, Peter Childers and Henry Finder, in helping to locate some of the critical material included in this book.

The introduction attempts to trace Heaney's development from his poetic origins through *North* and *Field Work*, while emphasizing the covert struggle with the dangerous influence of W. B. Yeats. William Bedford begins the chronological sequence of criticism in a shrewd review of *North*, which finds that Heaney's development away from a Yeatsian rhetoric is unfortunately also a falling away from an earlier passionate intensity. In an early consideration of Heaney's first three volumes, D. E. S. Maxwell more positively centers upon the poet's remarkable ability to enrich his tone by orchestrating it, without essentially altering his stance. Terence Brown, in another early survey, places particular stress upon hidden ambivalences in Heaney's work, especially in regard to that violence which has formed and continues to shape what might be called "the matter of Ireland."

The late Robert Fitzgerald, eminent poet and translator, in a pioneering American appreciation of Heaney, celebrates the Irish poet's "unforced audacity" and "distant tenderness." More detailed criticism may be said to begin with John Wilson Foster's investigation of motifs and sources in "A Lough Neagh Sequence," in Rita Zoutenbier's historical view of Heaney's relation to the matter of Ireland, and in P. R. King's careful tracing of the development of personal identity, with all its daunting complexities, in Heaney's poetry from its origins through *North*.

In a strong instance of American appreciation, the poet Jay Parini joins himself to Robert Fitzgerald as a celebrator of Heaney's labor of reclamation of the English lyric for Ulster. The British poet Anthony Thwaite, summing up Heaney's first decade of achievement (1965–1975), suggests the larger context of Wordsworthian tradition as being deeply relevant to our apprehension of the Irish poet. With Blake Morrison's informed analysis of *Field Work*, Heaney's best single volume to date, a salutary emphasis is placed upon the way in which Heaney has altered contemporary English poetry, turning it back to a greater rhetorical richness after the thinning out of the tradition by Philip Larkin and his followers.

Carlanda Green, surveying what she calls "the feminine principle" in Heaney's poetry, with its optimistic view of marriage, implicitly commends the poet for holding on to traditional views that many now would judge to be archaic. This book concludes with three recent reviews of the latest work by Heaney. Douglas Dunn, briefly commenting on both *Sweeney Astray* and *Station Island*, implicitly indicates his judgment that the poet necessarily remains distracted by the matter of Ireland, which thus interferes with his full development. In a commentary upon *Station Island*, our most eminent biographical critic, Richard Ellmann, writes out of the authority of being the definitive scholar of Wilde, Yeats, and Joyce. His judgment is that Heaney is more in Joyce's mode than in the line of Yeats, and he praises the "exfoliating and augmenting" of Heaney's "prodigious" talent in *Station Island*. Time must tell us if Ellmann is right, or if the editor's introduction, with its observations upon Heaney's inevitable agon with Yeats, will prove to be correct in the longer span. Helen Vendler, in the review of *Station Island* that concludes this volume, associates Heaney with Dante, thus following Heaney's own preference. Astute and subtle in her reading, Vendler, like Ellmann, may take Heaney too much at his own word, but that is another fitting critical tribute to Heaney's preternatural eloquence as a poet.

Introduction

At thirty-nine, Wallace Stevens wrote "Le Monocle de Mon Oncle"; at about the same age Yeats wrote "Adam's Curse." Texts of the fortieth year form a remarkable grouping; I can think immediately of Browning's "Childe Roland" and Poe's "Eureka," and I invite every reader to add more (Whitman's "Out of the Cradle" and "As I Ebb'd" suddenly come to mind, but there are many others). I would not say that the Northern Irish poet Seamus Heaney, at forty, has printed any single poem necessarily as fine as "Adam's Curse," but the lyric called "The Harvest Bow" in *Field Work* may yet seem that strong, against all of time's revenges. There are other poems in *Field Work* worthy of comparison to the Yeats of *In the Seven Woods* (1904), and it begins to seem not farfetched to wonder how remarkable a poet Heaney may yet become, if he can continue the steady growth of an art as deliberate, as restrained, and yet as authoritative and universal as the poems of *Field Work*—his fifth and much his best volume in the thirteen years since his first book, *Death of a Naturalist* (1966).

That book, praised for its countryman's veracity and vividness of soil-sense, reads in retrospect as a kind of dark hymn of poetic incarnation, a sombre record of the transgression of having been a Clare-like changeling. Heaney's first poems hold implicit his central trope, *the vowel of earth,* and move in a cycle between the guilt of having forsaken spade for pen, and the redemption of poetic work: "I rhyme. To see myself, to set the darkness echoing." *Door into the Dark* (1969) seems now, as it did to me a decade ago, mostly a repetition, albeit in a finer tone, and I remember putting the book aside with the sad reflection that Heaney was fixated in a rugged but minimalist lyrical art. I was mistaken and should have read more carefully the book's last poem, "Bogland," where Heaney began to open both to the Irish, and to his own abyss. Reading backwards from *Field Work* (and the

1

two other, intervening books) I am taught now by the poet how he passed from description to a visionary negation:

> Our pioneers keep striking
> Inwards and downwards,
>
> Every layer they strip
> Seems camped on before.
> The bogholes might be Atlantic seepage.
> The wet centre is bottomless.

Such a center indeed could not hold, and Heaney was poised upon the verge of becoming a poet of the Northern Irish Troubles, a role he now wisely seeks to evade, but in a morally rich sense of "evade," as I will try to show later. *Wintering Out* (1972) seems stronger than it did seven years ago, when it began to change my mind about Heaney's importance. It is a book about nearing the journey's center, and takes as its concern the poet's severe questioning of his own language, the English at once his own and not his own, since Heaney is of the Catholic Irish of Derry. Few books of poems brood so hard upon names, or touch so overtly upon particular words *as words*. No single poem stands out, even upon rereading, for this is the last volume of Heaney's careful apprenticeship as he works towards his deferred glory. *North* (1975) begins that glory, a vital achievement by any standards, perhaps a touch dimmed for American critics by the accident of its appearance so close to Geoffrey Hill's *Somewhere Is Such a Kingdom,* which gathered together in America Hill's first three volumes. But the power of *North* is that four years of reading have enhanced it, while *Field Work* seems to me the only recent British book of poems worthy of sustained comparison to the magnificence of Hill's *Tenebrae,* published in 1978.

Heaney's first three books sparred gently with local and contemporary precursors; the alert reader could find the colors and flavors of Kavanagh and Montague, of Ted Hughes and R. S. Thomas. Like the deliberate touches of the late Robert Lowell in *Field Work,* these are all "screen-memories," of interest only as tactical blinds. What emerges in *North,* and stands clear in *Field Work,* is the precursor proper, the middle Yeats, with whom the agon of the strong Irish poet must be fought, as much by Heaney in his maturity as it is by Kinsella, with the agon itself guaranteeing why Heaney and Kinsella are likely to become more memorable than Kavanagh and Clarke, among the Irish poets following Yeats.

I hear behind the poems of *North* the middle Yeats of *The Green Helmet* and of *Responsibilities,* a hearing reinforced by *Field Work*. This is the Yeats of a vision counting still its human cost, and so not yet abandoned to daemonic presences and intensities:

> I passed through the eye of the quern,
>
> Grist to an ancient mill,
> And in my mind's eye saw
> A world-tree of balanced stones,
> Querns piled like vertebrae,
> The marrow crushed to grounds.

That is Heaney's "Belderg" from *North,* but I do not think Yeats would have disowned it. The enduring poems in *North* include the majestic title-piece, as well as "Funeral Rites," "Kinship," "Whatever You Say Say Nothing," and, best of all, the sequence of poetic incarnation with the Yeatsian title, "Singing School." The poem "North" gave and still gives Heaney his poetics, as a mythic voice proclaims what must be this new poet's relation to the Irish past:

> It said, 'Lie down
> in the word-hoard, burrow
> the coil and gleam
> of your furrowed brain.
>
> Compose in darkness.
> Expect aurora borealis
> in the long foray
> but no cascade of light.
>
> Keep your eye clear
> as the bleb of the icicle,
> trust the feel of what nubbed treasure
> your hands have known.'

The reader of *Field Work* comes to realize that Heaney's eye is as clear, through discipline, as the air bubble in an icicle, as clear, say, as the American eye of the late Elizabeth Bishop. "Funeral Rites" inaugurates what seems doomed to be Heaney's central mode, whether he finally chooses Dublin or Belfast. "Kinship," a more difficult sequence, salutes the bog country as the "outback of my mind" and then flows into a grander trope:

> This is the vowel of earth
> dreaming its root
> in flowers and snow,
>
> mutation of weathers
> and seasons,
> a windfall composing
> the floor it rots into.
>
> I grew out of all this
> like a weeping willow
> inclined to
> the appetites of gravity.

Such inevitability of utterance would be more than enough if it were merely personal; it would suffice. Its grandeur is augmented in the last section of "Kinship" when Heaney acquires the authentic authority of becoming the voice of his people:

> Come back to this
> 'island of the ocean'
> where nothing will suffice.
> Read the inhumed faces
>
> of casualty and victim;
> report us fairly,
> how we slaughter
> for the common good
>
> and shave the heads
> of the notorious,
> how the goddess swallows
> our love and terror.

The problem for Heaney as a poet henceforward is how not to drown in this blood-dimmed tide. His great precedent is the Yeats of "Meditations in Time of Civil War" and "Nineteen Hundred and Nineteen," and it cannot be said in *North* that this precedent is met, even in "Whatever You Say Say Nothing," where the exuberance of the language achieves a genuine phantasmagoria. But "Singing School," with its queerly appropriate mix of Wordsworth and Yeats, does even better, ending poem and book with a finely rueful self-accepting portrait of the poet, still waiting for the word that is his alone:

I am neither internee nor informer;
An inner émigré, grown long-haired
And thoughtful; a wood–kerne

Escaped from the massacre,
Taking protective colouring
From bole and bark, feeling
Every wind that blows;

Who, blowing up these sparks
For their meagre heat, have missed
The once-in-a-lifetime portent,
The comet's pulsing rose.

That is true eloquence, but fortunately not the whole truth, as *Field Work* richly shows. Heaney is the poet of the vowel of earth and not of any portentous comet. In *Field Work,* he has gone south, away from the Belfast violence, heeding the admonition that Emerson addressed to himself in the bad year 1846, when the American slaveholders made war against Mexico:

Though loath to grieve
The evil time's sole patriot,
I cannot leave
My honied thought
For the priest's cant,
Or statesman's rant.

If I refuse
My study for their politique,
Which at the best is trick,
The angry Muse
Puts confusion in my brain.

Like Emerson, Heaney has learned that he has imprisoned thoughts of his own which only he can set free. No poem in *Field Work* is without its clear distinction, but I exercise here the critic's privilege of discussing those poems that move me most: "Casualty," "The Badgers," "The Singer's House," the lovely sequence of ten "Glanmore Sonnets," "The Harvest Bow" (Heaney's masterpiece so far), and the beautiful elegy "In Memoriam Francis Ledwidge," for the Irish poet killed on the Western Front in 1917. All of these lyrics and meditations practice a rich negation, an art of excluded meanings, vowels of earth almost lost between guttural consonants of history. Heaney's Irish sibyl warns him that "The ground we kept our

ear to for so long / Is flayed or calloused." The muted elegy "Casualty,"
which cunningly blends the modes of Yeats's "The Fisherman" and "Easter
1916," concludes in a funeral march giving us the sea's version of Heaney's
vowel of earth:

> They move in equal pace
> With the habitual
> Slow consolation
> of a dawdling engine,
> The line lifted, hand
> Over fist, cold sunshine
> On the water, the land
> Banked under fog: that morning
> I was taken in his boat,
> The screw purling, turning
> Indolent fathoms white,
> I tasted freedom with him.
> To get out early, haul
> Steadily off the bottom,
> Dispraise the catch, and smile
> As you find a rhythm
> Working you, slow mile by mile,
> Into your proper haunt
> Somewhere, well out, beyond . . .

Even as the slain fisherman's transcendence fuses with Heaney's catch
of a poem to send the poet also "beyond," so Heaney has revised Yeats's
ambition by having written an elegy as passionate as the perpetual night of
the Troubles. Even stronger is "The Badgers," an oblique poem of deepest
self-questioning, in which the elegiac strain is evaded and all simple meanings are thwarted. Sensing "some soft returning," whether of the murdered
dead or of the badgers, Heaney places upon his reader the burden of difficult interpretation:

> Visitations are taken for signs.
> At a second house I listened
> for duntings under the laurels
> and heard intimations whispered
> about being vaguely honoured.

The first line of this passage does not reach back to Lancelot Andrewes
through Eliot's "Gerontion" but rather itself boldly revises John 4 : 48,

"Except ye see signs and wonders, ye will not believe" and perhaps even Matthew 12 : 38–39. "An evil and adulterous generation seeketh after a sign." The duntings are at once the dull sounds of badgers and, more crucially, the Wordsworthian "low breathings" of *The Prelude* I, 323. Though an external haunting, testifying to the laurels of poetic election "vaguely honoured," they are also Heaney's hard-drawn breaths, in this text and out of it, in a murderous Northern Ireland. Heaney, once so ruggedly simplistic in his only apparent stance, has entered upon the agonistic way of a stronger poetry, necessarily denser, more allusive, and persuasively difficult.

I read this entrance as the triumph of "The Singer's House," a poem I will forebear quoting entire, though I badly want to, and give only the superb three stanzas of the conclusion, where Heaney laments the loss of everything in his land that should be "crystal," and discovers an inevitable image for his audacious and determined art that would reverse lament and loss:

> People here used to believe
> that drowned souls lived in the seals.
> At spring tides they might change shape.
> They loved music and swam in for a singer
>
> who might stand at the end of summer
> in the mouth of a whitewashed turf-shed,
> his shoulder to the jamb, his song
> a rowboat far out in evening.
>
> When I came here first you were always singing,
> a hint of the clip of the pick
> in your winnowing climb and attack.
> Raise it again, man. We still believe what we hear.

The verve of that final line is a tonic even for an American reader like myself, cut off from everything local that inspires and appalls Heaney. Closer to ordinary evenings in New Haven are the universal concerns that rise out of the local in the distinguished "Glanmore Sonnets" that open, again, with Heaney's central trope: "Vowels ploughed into other: opened ground." Confronting an image of the good life as field work, with art redeemed from violence and so "a paradigm" of new-ploughed earth, Heaney finds even in the first sonnet that his ghosts come striding back. Against the ghosts he seeks to set his own story as a poet who could heed Moneta's admonition to Keats, or Nietzsche's to all of us: "Think of the earth."

> Then I landed in the hedge-school of Glanmore
> And from the backs of ditches hoped to raise
> A voice caught back off slug-horn and slow chanter
> That might continue, hold, dispel, appease:
> Vowels ploughed into other, opened ground,
> Each verse returning like the plough turned round.

Yet the ninth sonnet is driven to ask with true desperation: "What is my apology for poetry?" and the superb tenth sonnet ends the sequence overtly echoing Wyatt's most passionate moment, while more darkly and repressively alluding to the Yeatsian insight of the perpetual virginity of the soul: "the lovely and painful / Covenants of flesh; our separateness." More hopeful, but with a qualified hope, is the perfect lyric "The Harvest Bow," which I quote in its entirety:

> As you plaited the harvest bow
> You implicated the mellowed silence in you
> In wheat that does not rust
> But brightens as it tightens twist by twist
> Into a knowable corona,
> A throwaway love-knot of straw.
>
> Hands that aged round ashplants and cane sticks
> And lapped the spurs on a lifetime of game cocks
> Harked to their gift and worked with fine intent
> Until your fingers moved somnambulant:
> I tell and finger it like braille,
> Gleaning the unsaid off the palpable,
>
> And if I spy into its golden loops
> I see us walk between the railway slopes
> Into an evening of long grass and midges,
> Blue smoke straight up, old beds and ploughs in hedges,
> An auction notice on an outhouse wall—
> You with a harvest bow in your lapel,
>
> Me with the fishing rod, already homesick
> For the big lift of these evenings, as your stick
> Whacking the tips off weeds and bushes
> Beats out of time, and beats, but flushes
> Nothing: that original townland
> Still tongue-tied in the straw tied by your hand.

The end of art is peace
Could be the motto of this frail device
That I have pinned up on our deal dresser—
Like a drawn snare
Slipped lately by the spirit of the corn
Yet burnished by its passage, and still warm.

Heaney could not have found a more wistful, Clare-like emblem than
the love knot of straw for this precariously beautiful poem, or a sadder,
gentler motto than: *"The end of art is peace."* Certainly the oversong of the
poem, its stance as love-lyric, seems to sing against Yeats's Paterian ringers
in the tower, who have appointed for the hymeneal of the soul a passing
bell. But the end of married love may be peace; the end of art is agonistic,
against time's "it was," and so against anterior art.

The hands which plait the harvest bow are masculine and hardened,
but delicate in the office of marriage, which brings in harvest. Implicated
in the making is the knowable corona of mellowed silence, not the unreli-
able knowledge of poetry; and Heaney as poet must both love and stand
back and away from this wisdom, paternal and maternal. The fingers which
follow a human tradition can move as if moving in sleep—"asleep in its
own life," as Stevens said of the child. But Heaney must "tell and finger
it like braille," for that is the poet's field of work: "Gleaning the unsaid
off the palpable," the slender pickings after the granary is full.

Though his vision, *through her emblem,* in the third stanza approximates a true peace, it breaks into something both richer and more forlorn
in what comes after. The young Yeats sang of "The Happy Townland,"
where "Boughs have their fruit and blossom / At all times of the year" and
"all that are killed in battle / Awaken to life again." Heaney, leaving
youth, hears in recollections of innocent venery a music that "Beats out of
time, and beats, but flushes / Nothing." There is nothing for it to start up
since the happy or original townland belongs only to those "still tongue-
tied" in the frail device of the harvest bow. Heaney's genius is never surer
than in his all-but-undoing of this emblem in his final trope, where the
love knot becomes a drawn snare recently evaded by the corn-king, an evasion that itself both burnishes and animates the knowable corona of
achieved marriage. Obliquely but firmly, the struggle of poetry displaces
the lover's stance, and the undersong finds a triumph in the poem's closure.

I verge upon saying that Heaney approaches the cunning stance of the
strong poet, evasion for which I cite not its American theorists and bards,
from Emerson through Whitman and Dickinson to Frost and Stevens but
the central British master of the mode:

> Know ye not then the Riddling of the Bards?
> Confusion, and illusion, and relation,
> Elusion, and occasion, and evasion?

That is Tennyson's Seer, not Emerson's Merlin, and must become Heaney's poetic, if like Yeats he is to transcend the vowel of earth. It will be a painful transition for a poet whose heart is with the visionary naturalism of Wordsworth and Keats and Clare (and Kavanagh, Montague, R. S. Thomas) rather than with a vision fighting free of earth. But there are signs in *Field Work* that the transition is under way. Heaney ends the book with a grim rendition of Dante's Ugolino, too relevant to the Irish moment, and with his not altogether successful title poem which invokes the Gnostic doubloon of Melville's Ahab. I end here by reading in the noble quatrains of Heaney's "In Memoriam Francis Ledwidge" a powerful evasion of a fate that this poet will never accept as his own:

> In you, our dead enigma, all the strains
> Criss-cross in useless equilibrium
> And as the wind tunes through this vigilant bronze
> I hear again the sure confusing drum
>
> You followed from Boyne water to the Balkans
> But miss the twilit note your flute should sound.
> You were not keyed or pitched like these true-blue ones
> Though all of you consort now underground.

Not my way to go, as Heaney tells us, for he is keyed and pitched unlike any other significant poet now at work in the language, anywhere. The strains criss-cross in him in so useful an equilibrium that all critics and lovers of poetry must wish him every cunning for survival. To this critic, on the other side of the Atlantic, Heaney is joined now with Geoffrey Hill as a poet so severe and urgent that he compels the same attention as his strongest American contemporaries, and indeed as only the very strongest among them.

WILLIAM BEDFORD

"To Set the Darkness Echoing"

With the publication of *North*, Heaney has given us both the most explicit formulation of his concern with language, and the richest fulfillment of that concern. From *Death of a Naturalist* onwards, the tension between art and reality was obvious, the language almost physically struggling to assert a mastery of form and metaphor over experience, as in "Digging," from *Death of a Naturalist*:

> The cold smell of potato mould, the squelch and slap
> Of soggy peat, the curt cuts of an edge
> Through living roots awaken in my head.
> But I've no spade to follow men like them.
>
> Between my finger and my thumb
> The squat pen rests.
> I'll dig with it.

or a poem such as "The Forge," from *Door into the Dark*. It was a tension persistently seen in the experience of natural life, but rendered in a language highly conscious of its cultural community, as in "An Advancement of Learning" and "Synge on Aran" from *Death of a Naturalist,* and "Rite of Spring" and "The Wife's Tale" from *Door into the Dark*. Indeed, if there was a recurring theme among critics, it was precisely that Heaney's language was so obviously conscious of its cultural community, and handled the tradition with an emphasis that sometimes amounted to clumsiness, as in the metaphorical and mythological densities of "Vision," from *Door into the Dark*:

From *Delta: A Literary Review* 56 (1977). © 1977 by *Delta*.

> Years
> Later in the same fields
> He stood at night when eels
> Moved through the grass like hatched fears
>
> Towards the water. To stand
> In one place as the field flowed
> Past, a jellied road,
> To watch the eels crossing land
>
> Re-wound his world's live girdle.
> Phosphorescent, sinewed slime
> Continued at his feet. Time
> Confirmed the horrid cable.

Wintering Out resolved many of Heaney's earlier linguistic problems, and also moved towards a clearer perception of what was to be the central theme of *North*. The language—

> Our guttural muse
> was bulled long ago
> by the alliterative tradition
> ("Traditions")

—was pared down to a skeletal minimum, and thus enabled to carry its metaphorical meanings with a much more assured, authoritative clarity:

> Some day I will go to Aarhus
> To see his peat-brown head,
> The mild pods of his eye-lids,
> His pointed skin cap.
> ("The Tollund Man")

It is a language constantly moving towards clarity and precision, a language claiming for the imagination the authority needed to deal with the horrors of experience, rather in the manner of Geoffrey Hill in "Funeral Music," and in "The Songbook of Sebastian Arrurruz":

> I piece fragments together, past conjecture
> Establishing true sequences of pain;
>
> For so it is proper to find value
> In a bleak skill, as in the thing restored:
> The long-lost words of choice and valediction.

"Establishing true sequences of pain" could be taken as the organising principle of *North*, the endeavour of the imagination—"In a bleak skill, as in the thing restored"—to give true meaning and value, in language, to chaotic experience. As Heaney says in his title poem, the integration of "violence and epiphany."

North is in two main parts, the second dealing in an almost discursive detail with the themes enacted in the first. "Whatever You Say Say Nothing" explores the case with which language can become cliché when faced with extremes of experience such as the terrorist campaign in Ulster:

> Who proved upon their pulses 'escalate',
> 'Backlash' and 'crack down', 'the provisional wing',
> 'Polarization' and 'long-standing hate'.

and again:

> 'Oh, it's disgraceful, surely, I agree,'
> 'Where's it going to end?' 'It's getting worse.'
> 'They're murderers.' 'Internment, understandably . . .'
> The 'voice of sanity' is getting hoarse.

In such a situation, the great risk is that language will act virtually as an anaesthetic, turning reality into imagination:

> There was that white mist you get on a low ground
> And it was déjà-vu, some film made
> Of Stalag 17, a bad dream with no sound.

An inversion where it becomes difficult deliberately so to distinguish clearly between cliché and serious question, solution and straightforward description:

> Is there a life before death? That's chalked up
> In Ballymurphy. Competence with pain,
> Coherent miseries, a bite and sup,
> We hug our little destiny again.

Here, the graffito "Is there a life before death?" remains both graffito and question and the colloquial "chalked up" both colloquial and literal. Perhaps the answer to "Is there a life before death?" lies in the *fact* of graffiti being "chalked up" all over the Province; there can't be much life, neither can there be much understanding, language having deteriorated into the clichés of political and journalistic evasion. Perhaps the whole Ulster dilemma is summed up in the last three lines of the poem:

> Competence with pain,
> Coherent miseries, a bite and sup,
> We hug our little destiny again.

The language here condenses national characteristics; the loquacious pub-
talk of "Coherent miseries, a bite and sup"; the Irish sense of their own
fate, "We hug our little destiny again"; the background of efficient but
lethal terrorism. This has the colloquial and rhetorical blend of Yeats, arising naturally out of the "gelignite and sten" reality the poet is attempting
to articulate.

And yet, even if the poem seems to be recognising the failure of language as a medium for handling such experience, the poet still asserts his
claim to our attention:

> Yet I live here, I live here too, I sing,

an insistence that is biographically enlarged in the sequence "Singing
School"—a reference no doubt, to Yeats's "Sailing To Byzantium." Here,
the opening quotations are significant. Heaney juxtaposes an extract from
Wordsworth's *The Prelude* with one from Yeats's *Autobiographies,* and in doing so acknowledges the tension that sustains *North.* From Wordsworth,
we have:

> and I grew up
> Fostered alike by beauty and by fear;

and from Yeats, the great Irish poet behind much of Heaney's work recalling his own dream of dying "fighting the Fenians." The sequence, present-
ing quite straightforwardly biographical information, illustrates the tension
of the language:

> Have our accents
> Changed? 'Catholics, in general, don't speak
> As well as students from the Protestant schools.'
> ("The Ministry of Fear")

of the political situation—as in "A Constable Calls" which describes the
fear felt by the Catholic child when a Protestant policeman made a routine
crop-checking call at his father's farm:

> He stood up, shifted the baton-case

> Further round on his belt,
> Closed the domesday book,
> Fitted his cap back with two hands,
> And looked at me as he said goodbye.

and in the final poem, "Exposure," the dilemma in which this leaves the
poet:

> I am neither internee nor informer;
> An inner émigré, grown long-haired
> And thoughtful; a wood-kerne
>
> Escaped from the massacre,
> Taking protective colouring
> From bole and bark, feeling
> Every wind that blows;
>
> Who, blowing up these sparks
> For their meagre heat, have missed
> The once-in-a-lifetime portent,
> The comet's pulsing rose.

The poem's immediate subject is a December evening's walk in Wicklow,
during which the poet hopes, then fails, to see the comet, Kohoutek.
Working figuratively, the point seems to be that the poet has missed some
superior opportunity for creation by virtue of the compromises the situation
has forced him to make:

> If I could come on meteorite!

he exclaims, instead of:

> blowing up these sparks
> For their meagre heat

But in fact, he has not:

> Instead I walk through damp leaves,
> Husks, the spent flukes of autumn
>
> Imagining a hero
> On some muddy compound,
> His gift like a slingstone
> Whirled for the desperate.

"Imagining a hero" instead of capturing "Those million tons of light" by
coming "on meteorite"; weighing and weighing / My responsible *tristia*"
instead of articulating the almost Platonic "diamond absolutes"; it is this
kind of failure, the poem implies, that causes the ultimate failure—to have
missed:

> The once-in-a-lifetime portent,
> The comet's pulsing rose.

although the poem never actually makes clear what this "pulsing rose" could have been. But that is not essential to our understanding. The metaphor must carry the weight of the meaning, as so often in Heaney's work, and we are left with a pregnantly satisfactory image of the poet's own sense of his failure.

But of course, to talk of failure without having defined the nature of the ambition is misleading. For if the failure is a failure of language, this is only necessarily so in relation to the scope of the ambition. To render out of "violence" an "epiphany" which will give meaning to that violence; to give meaning, in art, to the meaningless; that is the scope of Heaney's ambition in *North,* and if "Exposure" suggests that the attempt has been a failure, it is perhaps only a relative failure whose success can be seen in the quality of the attempt.

The themes explored in part 1 of *North* are presented within the framework of the Antaeus legend, a vivid analogy of the struggle for control of the land—

> The ground possessed and repossessed.
> ("Ocean's Love To Ireland")

—that brings historical perspective to the Ulster situation. Within this framework, the poet attempts to find some meaning in the wider problem of violent death, and takes as his most fertile imagery the bog-grave findings discussed and illustrated in P. V. Glob's *The Bog People.* Poems based on this material have appeared elsewhere—"The Tollund Man" in *Wintering Out,* for instance—but the finest handling of the theme comes in "The Grauballe Man" from *North.* In this poem, the language is reduced to an essential metaphorical description out of which the body arises with its immediate meaning:

> As if he had been poured
> in tar, he lies
> on a pillow of turf
> and seems to weep
>
> the black river of himself.

If there is a significance to be found in violent death, then perhaps it is— as Christians would argue—the good that sometimes comes out of it, but for the poet, even this need not be the justification for the attempt to render in words the unspeakable. The conclusion of the poem seems to be that the poet, in capturing the death in a poem—

> but now he lies
> perfected in my memory,
> down to the red horn
> of his nails

—has somehow created a positive value from disintegration. The death is

> hung in the scales
> with beauty and atrocity

which, in context, I take to mean art and reality. Art is:

> the Dying Gaul
> too strictly compassed
>
> on his shield,

and reality is:

> the actual weight
> of each hooded victim,
> slashed and dumped.

an interpretation which I think is emphasized in the placing of "actual"— the reality of the "hooded victim" balanced with "the Dying Gaul / too strictly compassed / on his shield." In a sense, of course, it is ridiculous to suggest that a successful work of art somehow compensates for suffering, but bearing in mind the historically ritual function of poetry, this is not what I take it that Heaney means. If art is a serious business, then the attempt to create order out of chaos does have some value. And certainly, order is an important element in the use to which Heaney is putting his language. The very act of refining one's language to a spare, metaphorical precision, is an act of order and therefore, in some obscure way, respect. Such language, in its quiet dignity, *is* a value, if only of respect for the suffering described. "The Grauballe Man," in the way that it has taken horror—

> I first saw his twisted face
>
> in a photograph,
> a head and shoulder
> out of the peat,
> bruised like a forceps baby.

—and turned this into a living beauty—

> As if he had been poured
> in tar, he lies
> on a pillow of turf
> and seems to weep
>
> the black river of himself.

—seems to me one of Heaney's finest poems, and an emphatic refutation of the sense of failure suggested by "Exposure."

But is "The Grauballe Man" characteristic of the achievement of *North?* The success of the collection depends almost entirely, for me, upon the achievement of the poems in part 1. Certainly, the refined use of language is sustained throughout, but Heaney has sacrificed a great deal of his former energy. However artificial the language of *Death of a Naturalist* and *Door into the Dark,* the process begun in *Wintering Out,* and perfected in *North,* has its problems. The poems in part 2, for instance, in their very success in showing the vulnerability of language to the pressures of cliché and journalism, run the risk of hardly surviving as poetry at all. The prosaic flatness of almost all the poems except "Exposure " throws a disproportionate weight upon what is being said—rather in the manner of much Augustan verse, and Wordsworth's *Lyrical Ballads*—and it is a weight that the somewhat commonplace political content cannot support.

Starkly and rigorously as the language controls the response, much of Heaney's earlier richness is gone, and with it those syntactical tensions and ambiguities that enable poets like Hopkins and Yeats to contain such varieties of vision within their poetic texture. Avoiding the risks of rhetoric, Heaney has sacrificed much of the passion Yeats managed to sustain in his own political poems, and although *North* is undoubtedly Heaney's finest collection, one must doubt whether this direction can be followed much further without a vital weakening of the poetic imagination.

D. E. S. MAXWELL

Heaney's Poetic Landscape

Seamus Heaney now has three collections: *Death of a Naturalist* (1966), *Door into the Dark* (1969), and *Wintering Out* (1972). Critics are supposed to be clamorous that a poet should develop—as MacNeice sardonically observed, such critics, to observe any development, "need something deeper than a well and wider than a church-door." Its publishers claimed for *Wintering Out* "a noticeable widening of his poetic landscape." The opinion, though disputed in some reviews of the volume, is well founded. *Wintering Out* draws out previous themes into new alignments; it takes up fresh verbal and imaginative ambits; it consistently implies from its sense-impressions, still robustly present, a mosaic of thought and feeling. The poems of his first volume are concerned, primarily, to register the energies of a scene in its physical being. There is certainly an emotional response to what is being observed; and a coalescing towards symbol; but sensuous observation is in command.

The habitat is rural, entered at one level, it seems, assured of kinship:

> By God, the old man could handle a spade.
> Just like his old man.

> Snug on our bellies behind a rise of dead whins

> The long grey tapes of roads that bind and loose
> Villages and fields in casual marriage.

The scenes, bred into the bone from childhood years, can riot in luxuriant growth and colour, like the "glossy purple clot" of the first blackberry, its

From *Two Decades of Irish Writing: A Critical Survey.* © 1975 by D. E. S. Maxwell. Carcanet Press, 1975.

flesh "sweet / like thickened wine"; the seasonal tasks reassuring and familiar, churning day or a potato digging:

> The rough bark of humus erupts
> knots of potatoes (a clean birth).

The kinship is fragile and misleading; Heaney's country life is neither
glossy nor Arcadian. The influence of natural objects can be as often as not
to inspire fear, revulsion, disillusionment. The naturalist whose "death"
gives the volume its title progresses from an uninstructed fascination with
"the warm thick slobber / Of frogspawn" in the flax-dam where blue bot-
tles "Wove a strong gauze of sound around the smell." Later, coming on
the "gross-bellied frogs," croaking in multitude, "The slap and plop were
obscene threats."

> gathered there for vengeance and I knew
> that if I dipped my hand the spawn would clutch it.

The blackberries betray their beauty, "A rat-grey fungus, glutting on our
cache"; churning is hard graft, blistering hands, souring the house; there
is a routine, but to the child frightening, violence, when Dan Taggart
drowned kittens, "Or with a sickening tug, pulled old hens' necks." "Sickening": a recurrent word.

The conclusion is throwaway—pests have no place on a farm. The
poet establishes "a dreaded / Bridgehead," as when in "An Advancement of
Learning," he stares out the rats he loathes. The uncomely is to be assimilated too: violence, menace, are inherent in the land, whether in its daily
occupations, or in a heritage of blood. In "At a Potato Digging," "Fingers
go dead in the cold," and memories stir of other, earlier deaths:

> Live skulls, blind-eyed, balanced on
> wild higgledy skeletons
> scoured the land in forty-five
> wolfed the blighted root and died.

The next poem, "For the Commander of the *Eliza*," is a mordant narrative
of an incident recorded in Cecil Woodham-Smith's *The Great Hunger*. Past
and present run together in a chiaroscuro of experience; the collection initi-
ates the poet's design, "to set the darkness echoing."

There is a tension, in Heaney, between the farm life natural to his
childhood, and the recognition that he has abandoned his father's ways, belonging and not belonging:

Between my finger and my thumb
The squat pen rests.
I'll dig with it.

His diction, in a way, reflects the tension. It draws, discreetly, on a vein of "country words"; "slabber," "muck," "crocks," "creel," "clabber"; and it complements them with a delicately sophisticated imagery: a river "wearing / A transfer of gables and sky"; "Sky is a tense diaphragm." Heaney controls an exceptional variety of words, and of line. Knowing his background as his father does, he disturbs in it also more distant echoes and reflections. *Door into the Dark* consolidates his statement.

Tangible reality does not lose its tenure. "The Outlaw" celebrates the workmanlike servicing performed by an unlicensed bull. "The Wife's Tale"—Frost-like in a way—intimates in a harvest incident a domestic relationship bound to the "here and now" of daily life. Even the poems where the exteriors do not hazard their density, though, are commonly elegies for occupations, observances, crafts, past or fated to pass: an abandoned stable, a blacksmith remembering hoofs on the street outside his forge, a thatcher recollected from the palmy days of his skill. Surfaces increasingly contrive underlayers of meaning: loss and continuity, the cycle of birth and death, the sexual antithesis.

Thus "Rite of Spring" represents a water pump, thawed out from its frozen angle at the end of winter, in a kind of orgasmic release: "Her entrance was wet, and she came." The voice of the speaker in "Mother" working at a pump, conceives of her chore in sexual references. The stream in "Undine" is a metaphor—"he dug a spade deep in my flank / And took me to him"—of the "subtle increase and reflection" of female response. These emblems of human encounters participate in the seasonal rhythms of salmon and eel (notably in "A Lough Neagh Sequence"). Their most moving expression is in "Elegy for a Still-Born Child," where the narrating voice moves at the end from the "wreath of small clothes, a memorial pram," to a journey whose imagery may question its desolation:

Past mountain fields, full to the brim with cloud,
White waves riding home on a wintry lough.

There are shadows in the apparent clarities of Robert Frost that we may recognize in Heaney. "The Plantation," towards the end of this volume, has the same kind of suggestiveness as "Stopping by Woods on a Snowy Evening." It is a fable of a threatening wood, "birch trees / Ghosting your bearings," deceptive, yet enticing "Past the picnickers belt." Within earshot of the road, it is beyond the road's definitions, offering as it perplexes the chance of discovery, "To be pilot and stray—witch, / Hansel and Gretel in one." The more literal landscapes of other poems fall into such equivocations, their contours dissolving. The seascape of "Girls Bathing," endlessly consuming itself, is like the flux of the years. In "The Peninsula," "horizons drink down sea and hill, / The ploughed field swallows the whitewashed gable." The poem's final sequence, in an intricately managed sentence, frames a stanza of close visualization within the cryptic interpretation of it:

Now recall

The glazed foreshore and silhouetted log,
That rock where breakers shredded into rags,
The leggy birds stilted on their own legs,
Islands riding themselves out into the fog

And drive back home, still with nothing to say
Except that now you will encode all landscapes
By this: things founded clean on their own shapes,
Water and ground in their extremity.

The final poem, "Bogland," is like "The Plantation," a compression of paradoxes which Heaney has placed in Ireland, though they are omnipresent: deep loughs which kill and preserve; an island looking outward to sea, and inexhaustibly in upon itself; a journey within that leads to common habitations:

Every layer they strip
Seems camped on before.
The bogholes might be Atlantic seepage.
The wet centre is bottomless.

Wintering Out takes as its Preface a poem from a sequence ("Whatever You Say Say Nothing") published in the *Listener,* expressly about the Northern Irish violence. The point of the Preface, and of the exclusion of its companion pieces, is that the collection is to be read with the present horrors as one of its loci; but only as one, and it may be, not a major one. The "common sound effect" of gelignite (a phrase from the *Listener* sequence) has a buried life in poems seemingly apart from it. "The Last Mummer," for example, portrays this representative of his dying art parading the suburbs, angry with frustration, and throwing stones at the houses.

Heaney comments, "I didn't mean this to be a poem about Northern Ireland, but in some way I think it is."

In "A Northern Hoard," five poems in part 1 of *Wintering Out,* the detail of riot, tribal hatreds, the "smeared doorstep" and the "lumpy dead," directly, though intermittently, surfaces. For Heaney, the mindless violence, eroding even personal love, means exile, ears stopped to the mandrake-shriek of roots torn up. "I deserted": but the defection is inconclusive, broken by fitful returns, neither return nor absence satisfying. The private torment shelves into and out from public views, each powerfully augmenting the other, of a fragmented society, hard and ravenous:

> flint and iron,
> Cast-offs, scraps, nail, canine.

The vistas of *Wintering Out* open directly on the present Northern violence. If the volume has a central question, it is that of Shakespeare's MacMorris, "What ish my nation?," turning for its answers to circumstances of which the present troubles are only one instance. Repeatedly here, Heaney invokes the rights and rites of language, in places whose names, English and not-English, pronounce a domicile: "*Anahorish,* soft gradient / of consonant, vowel-meadow"; "the tawny guttural water / spells itself: Moyola"; "Demesnes staked out in consonants." Language is divisive too: in Broagh, the final "*gh* the strangers found / difficult to pronounce"; a Protestant neighbour, with a biblical image, speaks a "tongue of chosen people"; McCracken's hanged body is "a swinging tongue." So language draws in a host of other memorials to a troubled inheritance of "vowels and history," where heir and outcast dispute their roles: "man-killing parishes."

The phrase is from "The Tollund Man," where Heaney finds outside Ireland an archetype of ceremonial dispossession. The preserved, sacrificial corpse is a "saint's kept body," germinal, an ancestor of

> The scattered ambushed
> Flesh of labourers,
> Stockinged corpses
> Laid out in the farmyards.

The Tollund Man assumes in death a "sad freedom." Visiting his homeland, though "Not knowing their tongue," the poet would confirm a kinship:

> I will feel lost,
> Unhappy and at home.

The theme unifies the collection, glancing, for instance, into three related poems which are allegories of love and rejection, selfish, tender, destructive: "Maighdean Mara" (the mermaid), "Limbo" and "Bye-Child." Formally, the poems move within a starker diction of "stones," "stubble," "rock," more elusive rhymes, manners of declaration whose design is to solicit inference. If, as Brian Friel suggests, every writer has one tune to sing, Heaney's orchestrations of his have progressively enriched it.

TERENCE BROWN

A Northern Voice

From the first, critics responded to Heaney's extraordinary gift for realising the physical world freshly and with vigorous, exact economy. Heaney can bring everyday natural events before his readers' eyes with such telling precision that his images are both recognition and revelation:

> Flint-white, purple. They lie scattered
> like inflated pebbles. Native
> to the black hutch of clay
> where the halved seed shot and clotted
> these knobbed and slit-eyed tubers seem
> the petrified hearts of drills. Split
> by the spade, they show white as cream.
>   ("At a Potato Digging")

> Right along the lough shore
> A smoke of flies
> Drifts thick in the sunset.
>
> They come shattering daintily
> Against the windscreen
> The grill and bonnet whisper
>
> At their million collisions.
>   ("At Ardboe Point")

It is a mistake, however, to think of Heaney as merely a descriptive

From *Northern Voices: Poets From Ulster.* © 1975 by Terence Brown. Gill and Macmillan and Rowman and Littlefield, 1975. Originally entitled "Four New Voices: Poets of the Present."

nature poet, endowed with unusual powers of observation. From the first his involvement with landscape and locale, with the physical world, has been both more personal and more remarkable in its implications than any mere act of observation and record could be. Heaney has himself spoken about his sense of the Irish landscape:

> If you're involved with poetry, you are involved with words, and words, for me, seem to have more nervous energy when they are touching territory that I know, that I live with. I don't think of it as the Irish landscape: I think of it as a place that I know is ordinary, and I can lay my hand on it and know it, and the words come alive and get a kind of personality when they're involved with it. In other words, the landscape, for me, is image, and it's almost an element to work with as much as it is an object of admiration or description.

The images here ("lay my hand on it and know it") are religio-erotic and serve as a guide to the kind of personality with which Heaney invests his language. For his poems on landscape, on natural events and activities, are metaphors of a personal, if rather limiting, vision of the world.

The natural world as re-created in the language of Heaney's art is a powerful organic presence, manifesting itself in his early poetry in rich, massive processes. The rhythmic and linguistic density of Heaney's early work suggests this, as poems of thick, clotted verbal texture achieve, despite their weight, an ebb and flow movement, an ongoing fertility, as if

> the warm thick slobber
> Of frogspawn that grew like clotted water
> In the shade of the banks
>   ("Death of a Naturalist")

was in fact an analogue of their life. Ooze, ripe fullness, rot, the squelch and splash of a waterlogged landscape are embodied in poems that relish words rich on the tongue, almost to the point of satiation, the glut before decay.

> A thick crust, coarse-grained as limestone rough-cast,
> hardened gradually on top of the four crocks
> that stood, large pottery bombs, in the small pantry.
> After the hot brewery of gland, cud and udder
> cool porous earthenware fermented the buttermilk
> for churning day, when the hooped churn was scoured

with plumping kettles and the busy scrubber
echoed daintily on the seasoned wood.

And in the house we moved with gravid ease,
our grains turned crystals full of clean deal churns,
the plash and gurgle of the sour-breathed milk,
the pat and slap of small spades on wet lumps.
                                        ("Churning Day")

For Heaney, the natural world must be accepted for what it is—heavy, palpable in its irrefutable bulk, in its almost intractable forms. He paints it in thick oils, rarely allowing (except in the delightful "Lovers on Aran") for light, fire, air, for what the poet has himself called "the sideral beauty" of things. This is a dawn sky:

Clouds ran their wet mortar, plastered the daybreak
Grey
                                        ("Dawn Shoot")

this a waterfall:

My eye rides over and downwards, falls with
Hurtling tons that slabber and spill,
Falls, yet records the tumult thus standing still.
                                        ("Waterfall")

Heaney's sense of landscape combines erotic and religious impulses. He responds with a deep sense of the numinous in the natural world, and reads a scene as if it were governed by feminine, sexual principles. He confesses himself open to "intuitions that relate human female psychology and sexuality to the landscape itself." So he often writes as if a woman were the landscape, while much of his landscape verse implicitly suggests feminine sexuality and fertility.

In Heaney's imagination, which is synthetic and osmotic (in the sense that ideas and intuitions seep across thin membranes to blend with each other), this sense of landscape and the natural world extends in its implications into his treatment of another major obsession—Irish history and mythology. The implications of his vision of landscape are that nature, for all its processes, is a static form shaped by feminine forces, worked on by energetic, crafty makers, diggers, ploughmen. Irish history, too, reveals itself in his poetry as a landscape, feminine, protective, preservative, in which man's artifacts and deeds are received in an embracing comprehension. Love for this deity induces dark fantasy and nightmare, drives to deeds of desperation. A more strictly historical intelligence than Heaney's moves to distinguish nature and history. Heaney, dominated by a sense of nature's powers, reads history, language, and myth as bound up with nature, with territory, and with landscape.

In developing his vision of Ireland as territory Heaney owes much to the work of the human geographer Estyn Evans, who has spent most of his academic life in Belfast, at Queen's University. Poems such as "Churning Day" and "Bog Oak," as John Wilson Foster has suggested, may well originate in Heaney's reading of Evans's books, *Irish Heritage* (1942) and *Irish Folk Ways* (1957), while the concern with locale as a determinant of consciousness is something Heaney shares with Evans. But the difference between their minds is important. Evans's is an historical intelligence, concerned with causes and effects, intent to discriminate between nature and history. He is governed by rational impulses and is disinclined to mythologise the Irish past. In his writings the Irish countryside, its superstitions, folk customs and obsessions are regarded in a clear, reflective, humanist light, so that his work suggests the intellectual groundwork not for Heaney's writings but for John Hewitt's quiet celebration of man in relation to the earth. Heaney reads Evans and turns down the light, allowing the geographer's material to inhabit darker regions of the imagination. He invests Evans's subject matter and insights with religous and mythological significance. Evans lacks the religious sense almost entirely, writing with calm, materialist lack of fear about man's relationship with his Irish environment. Heaney writes of that same relationship, but in fear and trembling, in religious humility. For he feels that in sensing a human relationship to landscape, we relate to darker, stranger energies that could enter, without disturbance, the calm, sane pages of Evans's discourse. In an interview Heaney has spoken of this natural-historical-religio-sexual complex which is his central imaginative obsession:

> The bogs in Northern Europe in the first and second centuries
> A.D. contained the shrines of the god—or the goddess of the
> time, and in order that the vegetation and community would
> live again after the winter human sacrifices were made, people
> were drowned in the bogs and they have found these people.
> Now Tacitus reports on this in his *Germania* and you have a so-
> ciety in Iron Age where there was ritual blood-letting and kill-
> ing to a goddess of the territory of the ground. You have a soci-
> ety where girls' heads were shaved for adultery, you have a

religion centering on the territory, on a goddess of the ground and of the land and associated with sacrifice. Now in many ways the fury of Irish Republicanism is associated with a religion like this, with a female goddess who has appeared in various guises. She appears as Cathleen Ni Houlihan in Yeats's play; she appears as Mother Ireland, she appears you know playing her harp. I think that the kind of republican ethos is a feminine religion in a way. . . . It seems to me that there are satisfactory imaginative parallels between this religion and time and our own time, and it is observed with amazement and a kind of civilized tut-tut by Tacitus in the first century A.D. and by leader-writers in the *Daily Telegraph* in the twentieth century.

Heaney has explored these parallels between prehistory's feminine territorial religion that demanded human sacrifice, and Ulster's contemporary violence, through a sequence of poems which relate the recently discovered bodies of sacrificial victims in a bog in Denmark (Heaney learnt of these in P.V. Glob's book *The Bog People*) to recent republican atrocities. "The Tollund Man" associates the victim of a fertility cult with political murder in Ireland's Civil War, evoking each with religio-sexual metaphors:

> Bridegroom to the goddess,
>
> She tightened her torc on him
> And opened her fen,
> Those dark juices working
> Him to saint's kept body.
>
> I could risk blasphemy,
> Consecrate the cauldron bog
> Our holy ground and pray
> Him to make germinate
>
> The scattered, ambushed
> Flesh of labourers,
> Stockinged corpses
> Laid out in the farmyards,
>
> Tell-tale skin and teeth
> Flecking the sleepers
> Of four young brothers, trailed
> For miles along the lines.

"Punishment," a later, uncollected poem, further exploits such analogies as a drowned female corpse, an Iron Age adulteress, is lovingly contemplated as kin of more recent victims of the goddesses' expiatory hunger:

> I who have stood dumb
> as your betraying sisters,
> cauled in tar,
> wept by the railings,
>
> would connive
> in civilised outrage
> yet understand the exact
> and tribal, intimate revenge.

With Irish history controlled by such a demanding deity, it is not surprising to find that Heaney has little sense of change. For him, as for Montague, for Fiacc, and for the revival poets, history is a saga whose plot is the manifest appearance of a dark permanence of ancient forms. So Heaney, peering into the well of the past, deep into the bog of Irish racial consciousness, can question as he prospects "what new / in a hundred centuries' / loam":

> I push into a souterrain
>
> till I am sleeved in
>
> alluvial mud that shelves
> suddenly under
> bogwater and tributaries,
> and elvers tail my hair.
>
> ("Toome")

The bog is the primary reality, receiving, preserving, so that history is a laying down of strata in a developing landscape whose form was determined in prehistory. The social landscape is enriched or complicated by the strata, as they are laid down by invasion and by linguistic and racial complication, but the fundamental structure remains the same.

Thus many of Heaney's more recent poems are, in his own term, "Soundings": "*Soundings* can mean two things: the activity of taking readings of the sea's depth and the area within which this activity is possible. It implies a notion of geographical limits and of exploration of depth within those limits." These poems examine the dimensions and the texture of various layers of Ireland's experience, often concentrating on the linguistic constituents of the country's complex geological formation. Place-names encourage reflections on the rich compost which is language in Ireland:

> Soft voices of the dead
> are whispering by the shore
>
> that I would question
> (and for my children's sake)
> about crops rotted, river mud
> glazing the baked clay floor.
>
> The tawny guttural water
> spells itself: Moyola
> is its own score and consort,
>
> bedding the locale
> in the utterance,
> reed music, an old chanter
>
> breathing its mists
> through vowels and history.
> ("Gifts of Rain")

Sometimes a word, a flavour on the tongue, will provoke images of Gaelic purity—the neo-pastoral, Edenic vision briefly enchants the poet, as in "Anahorish":

> My 'place of clear water',
> the first hill in the world
> where springs washed into
> the shiny grass . . .

At other moments the poet is drawn to Elizabethan or to eighteenth-century, bourgeois Ireland as soft names "like Bruges" bring to mind

> a language of water wheels,
> A lost syntax of looms and spindles.
> ("The Wool Trade")

Elsewhere the natural world itself brings a lost language to mind in a reversal of this process, as when in "The Backward Look"

> A snipe's bleat is fleeing
> its nesting ground

into dialect,
into variants.

A poem such as "Bog Oak" in *Wintering Out* (1972), Heaney's third volume, is characteristic of these poems in which history seems a timeless present, a geological formation composed of many elements, open at moments to inspection at one of its levels, where each stratum implies the whole. The past, to change the metaphor, is a sequence of notes in a scale; the poet, as chance offers opportunity, strikes one experimentally and listens as the resonant harmonics sound. So the poem opens as the poet contemplates "A carter's trophy / split for rafters." This stirs into the consciousness an imagery of Ireland's suffering peasantry—"the moustached / dead, the creel-fillers"—and of rural deprivation:

> a blow-down of smoke
> struggles over the half-door
>
> and mizzling rain
> blurs the far end
> of the cart track.

The poem then cross-fades to highlight the contrast between the Irish landscape and social conditions which the poet describes and the English and European experience:

> The softening ruts
>
> lead back to no
> 'oak groves', no
> cutters of mistletoe
> in the green clearings.

Tacitus would have spoken of oak groves; a sun-warmed, pagan culture is implied in the imagery of mistletoe and clearings. Neither is native to Ireland's wilder, more bitter experience. So the poet turns to imagine Edmund Spenser in Ireland, representative of classical and Romance culture, "dreaming sunlight" as he watches the native population creep, after the Battle of Kinsale, "out of every corner / of the woodes and glennes" (the phrase is in fact Spenser's from his *Veue of the Present State of Ireland*) towards the only mode of survival open to a conquered people—"watercress and carrion."

Heaney's sense of the self and of the poetic imagination is markedly similar to his apprehension of nature and history. He himself has remarked, indeed, that in Ireland "our sense of the past, our sense of the land and perhaps even our sense of identity are inextricably interwoven." So the imagination has its dark bog-like depths, its sediments and strata from which images and metaphors emerge unbidden into the light of consciousness. In "Personal Helicon" the self is a dark well in which the poet rhymes to see himself "to set the darkness echoing." In "Setting," Poem 4 of "A Lough Neagh Sequence,"

> A line goes out of sight and out of mind
> Down to the soft bottom of silt and sand

but also, one feels, to the bottom of the self. "The Plantation" manifests a level of consciousness from which the poet warns:

> You had to come back
> To learn how to lose yourself

while in "Toome" the poet pushes down "under the dislodged / slab of the tongue" into history and the alluvial mud of the self. Such a sense of self as bound up with, and almost indistinguishable from, the dense complex of Irish natural and historical experience, obviously allows Heaney to explore Ulster's contemporary social and political crisis through attending to his own memories and obsessions. Ireland and her goddess of territory shaped unchangeable patterns in the prehistories of landscape and of the self. History and experience lay strata upon strata, and the poet takes his soundings. So poems such as "The Other Side" and "A Northern Hoard" consider the poet's personal life, his recollections and nightmares, as moments when Irish reality becomes explicit in himself. In an interview with Harriet Cooke the poet testified to his sense of "deposits lying there" within the self, and in speaking with Patrick Garland he explained: "My view and way with poetry has never been to use it as a vehicle for making statements about situations. The poems have more come up like bodies out of the bog of my own imagination." What is most interesting about these remarks is their curious passivity, implying the existence of a self already formed before the poet turns to it for his subject matter, just as nature and history are permanent forms to which he may also turn.

The formal development of Heaney's poetry relates to this passive sense of life. His first poems, rich in texture and heavy with the weight of language and rhythm, established a vision of reality as a palpable intractable absolute from which the poet, the conscious self, must accept what gifts may come. His recent poetry is more spare, the lines less loaded with poetic and linguistic ore; these poems are moments of revelation when the past, the land and the imagination permit insight into their packed depths. Where Heaney's early poems attempted to comprehend the whole of their experiences in crowded, apparently unselective, sensuously inclusive poetic organisms, his recent poems seem the minimal revelations of a reality that exists at the beck and call of no man—not even of the poet.

An impression of poetic and imaginative humility is one of these poems' initially attractive features. Yet it is this very humility, which one suspects in fact may be a quietist acquiescence, a passivity before the goddess, that this reader finds unsatisfying in Heaney's work, confining its emotional and dramatic possibilities. Heaney has in a singularly beautiful phrase defined a poem as "a completely successful love act between the craft and the gift." He clearly thinks that a poem comes up out of the dark, almost unbidden, organically oozing up through capillary channels pressured by incomprehensible forces. He contrasts this to what he considers a "more Yeatsian view of poetry":

> When he talked about poetry, Yeats never talked about the 'ooze' or 'nurture'. He always talked about the 'labour' and the 'making' and 'the fascination of what's difficult'.

Elsewhere Heaney has spoken further on the nature of the poetic act. He sees the writing of successful poetry as an effect of technique which means "being able to conduct yourself between the dark and the light in your head, not trusting or committing yourself to one or the other. . . . I think there . . . has to be a kind of soft retentive listening in your imagination and at the same time some kind of forceful technical craft-ridden action."

In all these remarks and in poems such as "The Thatcher" and "The Forge" poetry is seen as a technique whereby the artist applies crafty and traditional skills to given material. Nowhere is there any suggestion that the poet must shape his own materials, must make and remake himself, determining through hard intellectual labour what self his poetry will embody. In writing of the Yeatsian view of poetry, therefore, Heaney attaches the Yeatsian terms "labour," "making," "the fascination of what's difficult" to his own term, "craft." But for Yeats "labour" was as much the arduous task, between poems, of remaking over and over again his poetic, imaginative self, as it was concern with rhyme and rhythms. For Yeats the self was not an intractable absolute but a field of possibilities among which the poet is forced to choose, the drama of the choice itself being charged with poetic opportunity.

There is evidence in Heaney's work that such knowledge of the poetic self has not yet been achieved. The poems often give the impression that

Heaney has not decided fully what his feelings about the matter of his poetry could be. Choice of either a consistent or a dramatically inconsistent
stance within a poem is avoided in an indirection which, however admirable it may be with regard to journalistic exploitation of Ulster's present
troubles, renders much of his recent work gnomic and, in some instances,
emotionally ambiguous to the point where feeling itself drains from the
poems. At moments Heaney himself seems aware that his poetry avoids
choices, since he occasionally dramatises himself in positions of hesitating
indecision. "The Forge," for example, ends wih the poet still at the door
of the forge. "The Other Side" has the poet, at its conclusion, pondering:

> Should I slip away, I wonder,
> or go up and touch his shoulder
> and talk about the weather
>
> or the price of grass-seed?

while even "The Tollund Man" reaches an emotional climax with the
phrase "I could risk blasphemy" in circumspect affirmation.

Heaney does, of course, have emotions and attachments. It is rather
that he does not always appear willing to commit himself to them, possibly
because he is unsure what they in fact are or what they imply. His recent
poetry has therefore seemed at times a remarkably skilled, compelling poetic organisation of his indecision, lacking emotional range and drama.

The emotions that I detect running underground through Heaney's
work, emotions that have surfaced only once or twice as the subjects of
poems, are feelings of revulsion and attraction to violence, pain, and death.
These are often implicit in the poet's images where empathetic identifi-
cations with victims' shame or with oppressors' sadistic sensations are persistent features. In "The Barn" the poet declares: "I was chaff / To be
pecked up when birds shot through the air-slits." "The Early Purges" offers
a glimpse of rotting corpses, "three sogged remains." "Mid-Term Break"
shows us a small boy dead "Paler now, / Wearing a poppy bruise on his
left temple." "At a Potato Digging" employs an imagery that anticipates
the psychological tensions of the Bog People sequence:

> Mouths tightened in, eyes died hard,
> faces chilled to a plucked bird.
> In a million wicker huts
> beaks of famine snipped at guts.

"Turkeys Observed" is dominated by a victim's feeling of shame and naked
vulnerability:

Blue-breasted in their indifferent mortuary,
Beached bare on the cold marble slabs
In immodest underwear frills of feather.

The fuselage is bare, the proudwings snapped,
The tail-fan stripped down to a shameful rudder.

Such identification with a victim's shame and suffering is implicit when the
poet sees a waterfall:

water goes over
Like villains dropped screaming to justice.
("Waterfall")

In "Dream" the poet is openly executioner:

I was hacking a stalk
Thick as a telegraph pole.

The next stroke
Found a man's head under the hook.
Before I woke
I heard the steel stop
In the bone of the brow.

In "The Salmon Fisher to the Salmon" the speaker informs his victim:
"You can't resist a gullet full of steel," while in poems such as "Undine,"
"Mother," "At Ardboe Point" and "Roots" sexuality and violence or death
exist in close relationship. In "Land," a poem rich in sexual implications,
the poet concludes, ear to the earth, in a strange love act:

If I lie with my ear
in this loop of silence

long enough, thigh-bone
and shoulder against the phantom ground,

I expect to pick up
a small drumming

and must not be surprised
in bursting air

to find myself snared, swinging
an ear-ring of sharp wire.

It is of course in the Bog People poems that Heaney consciously begins to express his feelings of identification with victims and their shame,
and with the agents of their indignity. So in "Punishment" the poet is
within the victim's consciousness:

> I can feel the tug
> Of the halter at the nape
> Of her neck, the wind
> On her naked front

while in "The Tollund Man" the poet reflects:

> Something of his sad freedom
> As he rode the tumbril
> Should come to me, driving,
> Saying the names
>
> Tollund, Grabaulle, Nebelgard,

In one poem, "Summer Home," Heaney allows such feelings as sadistic cruelty and masochistic ambivalence about pain to serve as the explicit
matter of his work. The poem is one of his finest so far. Here the poet
knows what his feelings are, recognises they are bitter and dark, yet risks
making a poem of them. The result is "an entire curve of emotion from
premonition through revulsion, placation, passion and recrimination to the
final chastened assertion." Such a poem emerges not from the impersonal
unconscious but from the pain and complexity of experience which the poet
has accepted as his proper territory. This poem is no corpse from the bog,
no gift from a dark goddess passively accepted by a craft-conscious artist.

> My children weep out of the hot foreign night.
> We walk the floor, my foul mouth takes it out
> On you and we lie stiff till dawn
> Attends the pillow, and the maize, and vine
> That holds its filling burden to the light.
> Yesterday rocks sang when we tapped
> Stalactites in the cave's old, dripping dark—
> Our love calls tiny as a tuning fork.

The final image here has the exciting inevitability that characterises the
truly original poem. At such a moment Heaney suggests that he is entering
into his full poetic powers and that he may become a poet of the first rank.

ROBERT FITZGERALD

Seamus Heaney: An Appreciation

In one of Seamus Heaney's poems, a fiddler is said to have gone alone to a stone hut on the most westerly of the Blasket Islands and there to have got a new air "out of the night."

> The house throbbed like his full violin.
> So whether he calls it spirit music
> Or not, I don't care. He took it
> Out of wind off mid-Atlantic.

"The Given Note," this poem is called. The fiddler's gale-given air stands for gifts of that kind in general, the *données* of imagination, and you can call them spirit music or not so long as by your choice you mean to take them seriously. Heaney's way of taking them has been staunch, responsible, watchful, and easy. His range has widened through four books in the last ten years until with *North*, his latest, old and new gifts are astringently and powerfully realized. There is no point in avoiding the inevitable comparison. Yeats is hardly a presence in his work—although there are two allusions that I will come to—but Heaney has heard a spirit music no less distinct than that of his great predecessor.

> John Synge, I and Augusta Gregory, thought
> All that we did, all that we said or sung
> Must come from contact with the soil, from that
> Contact everything Antaeus-like grew strong.

So Yeats reflected in one of his late poems, "The Municipal Gallery Revisited." And yet in truth very little that Yeats said or sang came from contact with the soil of Ireland in any literal sense; had he ever had his hands

---

From *The New Republic* (March 27, 1976). © 1976 by The New Republic, Inc.

in it? It is primary with Heaney that he has. His first sensory world was that of farm life in Derry, one of the northern-most counties of Northern Ireland. His poems were and are grounded in that land and its working: rituals and implements of farming, beasts of stockyard and stable, laboring muscles in arms and legs: the contours, odors, crops, and weathers of the earth. In his 20s he began to find an accurate language, weighted and spare, for a physical universe as intensely given as that of some Ionian speculator pairing, in his wonderment, rough and smooth, soft and hard, dry and moist, hot and cold . . .

Thence, and tenacious thereof, the life of the mind. Heaney's Irish landscape flickered and reeked from the start with sensibility and a sense of the past, with pathos, fantasy, and fear. "The Barn" begins:

> Threshed corn lay piled like grit of ivory
> Or solid as cement in two-lugged sacks.

But some gifts of imagination are fearsome. The poem comes in the end to a child's hallucinated fright:

> I lay face-down to shun the fear above.
> The two-lugged sacks moved in like great blind rats.

Heaney entitled his first book in 1966 *Death of a Naturalist,* after a poem in which the naturalist, a schoolboy collector of frogspawn from a flax dam, encounters there one day a conclave of bull frogs that terrify him:

> The great slime kings
> Were gathered there for vengeance . . .

"[S]lime kings . . . vengeance . . .". The event might seem little more than a wry memory were it not for the reverberation of these words in Heaney's later work; the place he gave the poem turned out to be prophetic.

Formally simple and conversational, a little clumsy and thick-tongued, Heaney's early poems were carefully guarded against the curse of lilt. None approached the summits of Irish poetry after Yeats, which I take to be Thomas Kinsella's beautiful and bitter "Country Walk" (1962) and "Down Stream" (1964). But Heaney had a deeper affinity than Kinsella for their common progenitor in Irish writing, Joyce. His work was and would be incarnational, conceived in an objective and substantial world and embodied in forms respectful of it, no matter how various with learning and linguistic art the music of the spirit might become. For such a writer a good poem can be autotelic and autonomous only after a manner of speaking, for it owes its life above all to the life of men and only necessarily, if you like, to the life of poetry; it is utterance and artifact on equal terms.

In Heaney's second book, *Door into the Dark* (1969) a shorter line, a more selective eye and ear were at work, as for instance to evoke an empty stall and a vanished plow horse:

> Green froth that lathered each end
> Of the shining bit
> Is a cobweb of grass-dust.

In this book, too, the given note more often had a carrying power beyond local matters. "Shoreline" is a good example. Here the visible and audible meeting of land and water all around Ireland, and within Ireland (has air travel given us eyes for this?) makes a wide scene held long in the mind, long enough to take in images and noises of beachings long ago, echoing finally in Viking and Norman place names. The poet now can work with bare but telling items in prose rhythms quietly spaced and ordered; he commands a style. He will extend it. Without strain the voice of "Shoreline" can call up, in his third book, *Wintering Out*, mythical and magical presences, derived no more from folklore than from experience. Poems such as "The Last Mummer" and "Maighdean Mara" are all of a piece with invocations of history like the more recent "Ocean's Love to Ireland."

I admire the unforced audacity and the tart, distant tenderness of this poem. An incident out of Aubrey's *Brief Lives*—Raleigh's rape of one of the Queen's maids of honor, whose alarmed "Sweet Sir Walter!" soon became incoherent—provides a figure for England and Ireland in the sixteenth century, but the possessor is at once tidal and oceanic even while remaining Elizabeth's courtier and soldier, and the still richer details of part 3 come together to state something with great precision that would be unstatable otherwise. The poet disposes of twentieth-century poetic means, as in the quotations chosen and placed with more than Poundian ebullience and force. But a kind of courtesy regulates Heaney's writing. In the Age of Criticism the cultivation of poetry as a superior amusement, superior indeed in the work of at least one master, has gone so far among later talents as to attenuate and trivialize the whole business. Heaney's best poems in their purity are certainly fresh esthetic objects; at the same time his manner is large and open, his intent a publicly conducted meditation among the living and the dead.

Two poems in *North* suggest, at least partially, Heaney's poetics. In the title poem he hears the "ocean-deafened voices" of old fabulous raiders saying to him:

> Lie down
> in the word-hoard, burrow
> the coil and gleam
> of your furrowed brain.
>
> Compose in darkness.
> Expect aurora borealis
> in the long foray
> but no cascades of light.
>
> Keep your eye clear
> as the bleb of the icicle,
> trust the feel of what nubbed treasure
> your hands have known.

In another and longer, "Bone Dreams," he recalls finding the Anglo-Saxon *ban-hus* for body.

> Bone-house:
> a skeleton
> in the tongue's
> old dungeons.
>
> I push back
> through dictions,
> Elizabethan canopies,
> Norman devices,
>
> the erotic mayflowers
> of Provence
> and the ivied latins
> of churchmen
>
> to the scop's
> twange, the iron
> flash of consonants
> cleaving the line.

There are moments of delicate erotic or "ivied" music in these poems. But the old languages, Irish, Norse, Anglo-Saxon, have reinforced Heaney's ruggedness, a quality not only of vocabulary but of mood and temper upon which the poet had occasion to depend.

> Out of Ireland we come.
> Great hatred, little room,
> Maimed us at the start.

wrote Yeats in 1931. One of Heaney's two allusions to that master is the title "Singing School" for a group of poems in part 2 of *North,* all concerned with the orientation of a Catholic poet amid the pressures of life in Northern Ireland before and after the eruption of killing in the summer of 1969. To enlarge on the irony of the title he quotes as one epigraph a few sentences from Yeats' *Autobiographies* remembering how a stable boy's "book of Orange rhymes" put it into his head as a child that he "would like to die fighting the Fenians." The other epigraph is Wordsworth's "I grew up / Fostered alike by beauty and by fear." In the fourth poem of this group, called "Summer of 1969," Heaney recalls hearing the news from Belfast in Madrid and concludes with Goya's images in the Prado:

> His nightmares, grafted to the palace wall—
> Dark cyclones, hosting, breaking; Saturn
> Jewelled in the blood of his own children,
> Gigantic Chaos turning his brute hips
> Over the world. Also that holmgang
> Where two berserks club each other to death
> For honor's sake, greaved in a bog, and sinking.

Here is the customary exertion of strength and precision in diction.

A holmgang is a single combat on an island. Two more lines frame the images, but I have not quoted them because to my ear they detract from the power of this borrowing as a commentary on events in Northern Ireland. In other poems self-questioning, sorrow, fierce irritation and disgust can enter the speaking voice:

> Long sucking the hind tit
> Cold as a witch's and as hard to swallow
> Still leaves us fork-tongued on the border bit:
> The liberal papist note sounds hollow
>
> When amplified and mixed in with the bangs
> That shake all hearts and windows day and night.

Door into the Dark included a short poem, "Bogland," in homage to the Irish peat bogs in which archaeological finds have been made from prehistoric and historic times: the skeleton of the Great Irish Elk, for example. But it was somewhat later and through a book by the Danish archaeologist

P. V. Glob that the North European boglands took hold of Heaney's imagination and supplied him with a master image or metaphor. Bogwater may
be so preservative that anything lost—or deposited—in it will decompose
little for centuries. In the peat bogs of northwest Europe hundreds of human bodies have been found, many of them Iron Age people, often stran-
gled victims of human sacrifice or punishment. Some of these *objets trouvés*
are charged with frightful and monumental beauty: the Tollund Man and
the Grauballe Man in Jutland, the "Viking Queen" in County Armagh.
Pondering these, Heaney made eight poems like found objects themselves.
Here contact with the soil meant contact through the familiar peat bogs
with ancient depths of European life, tribal, pre-Christian and indeed pre-
Roman (though relevant notes could be found in Tacitus). Heaney tried a
"refraction" of Northern Irish murderousness in the perspective these
depths, and the earth itself, afforded. . . . "This centre holds," Heaney's
other allusion to Yeats, appears as the first line of part 4 [of "Kinship"]
and makes explicit in passing the reserve toward Yeats that all his work
implies. Elsewhere he has said, "the language and landscape of
Ireland . . . can be regarded as information retrieval systems for their own
history: the bog bank is a memory bank." As a figure for the memory of a
people his bogland is literally more down-to-earth than Yeats' *anima mundi*.
And what Denis Donoghue said of Yeats—that he "invented a country,
calling it Ireland"—cannot be said of the younger poet.

Heaney's piety toward the life of his boyhood appears in two excellent,
comparatively late poems, "Sunlight" and "A Drink of Water." But his
tribal sense, his learning, and his imagination have collaborated most remarkably, perhaps, in the poem "Funeral Rites." Here he envisages for the
dead-by-violence a ceremony on a grand scale and a glimpse of heroic ap-
peasement. The "great chambers of Boyne" are the megalithic tombs at
New Grange, to which you drive from Belfast through the Gap of the
North, skirting loughs with Scandinavian names. Gunnar is a figure out
of Icelandic saga at whose burial a cycle of vengeance was broken, at least
temporarily, by a miracle of strange light and happiness beyond death. It
is almost startling to think that the measured progression and elevation of
this poem can do nothing for Northern Ireland.

JOHN WILSON FOSTER

"A Lough Neagh Sequence":
Sources and Motifs

"A Lough Neagh Sequence" occupies the poetic center of Seamus Heaney's second volume, *Door into the Dark* (1969). A seven-part poem, it gathers and interrelates the chief motifs of the entire book and, arguably, of *Death of a Naturalist* (1966) as well—darkness, descent, and homing, the latter two punningly contained in the word "gravitate," a variant of which Heaney exploits in "Gravities" from *Death of a Naturalist*. "A Lough Neagh Sequence" taxed Heaney's powers of design more than any poem up until then, though such powers have subsequently found greater play, but no greater compactness, in *Wintering Out* (1972) and *North* (1975).

Almost as interesting as Heaney's achievement of design is the manner in which Heaney appropriates in "A Lough Neagh Sequence" both scientific knowledge of the eel and the superstition that surrounds the fish in Ulster and abroad. Clearly, some of this lore is derived from direct acquaintance in the field, for the poet hails from the countryside rimming the Derry shores of Lough Neagh. Equally clearly, some is derived from literature on the eel. Latter-day scientific sources of "A Lough Neagh Sequence" are unknown, and do not matter, but we do know of one nineteenth-century source. The sequence was published separately by the Phoenix Pamphlet Poets Press (Manchester, 1969) and had as epigraphs two quotations from *The Fishes of Great Britain and Ireland*, 2 vols. (London, 1880–84), by Francis Day. Scientific in intent, Day's book nonetheless discusses the superstitions surrounding the eel throughout history, perhaps in

From *Éire-Ireland* 12, no. 2 (1977). © 1977 by the Irish American Cultural Institute. Originally entitled "Seamus Heaney's 'A Lough Neagh Sequence': Sources and Motifs."

an attempt to bridge the sizeable gaps in contemporary biology of the eel. At any rate, Day's work can be said to have safely passed into booklore and scientific history.

So, too, though still readable and valuable, can the sources Day drew heavily upon, the writings of the eminent Ulster zoologists, William Thompson and Robert Patterson. As pioneers, a quarter century before Day, in the effort to push back the frontier of knowledge about the eel, Thompson and Patterson were able to make direct observations in Heaney country around Toomebridge and along the river Bann as well as to record the regional folk beliefs and yarns about this mysterious fish. Although the poet may not know it, some of the ichthyology and folklore in "A Lough Neagh Sequence" is appropriately traceable, demonstrably and conjecturally, to the work of Patterson and Thompson.

"A Lough Neagh Sequence" interweaves an account of the eel's life cycle with an account of how the lough fishermen catch the fish. The first poem of the sequence, "Up the Shore," immediately registers the major legends of the lough as well as the power of its dark deeps to absorb and preserve like a bog, hardening wood to stone, or—as Heaney has it in "Relic of Memory," the poem preceding the sequence in *Door into the Dark*—incarcerating ghosts and stunning stakes to stalagmites. Up the shore from the commercial weirs, the local fishermen harvest the eel, and in doing so brave a small matter of destiny. The lough has the gravitational pull of the dark and primal origins, which the fishermen laconically acknowledge when they refuse to learn to swim, remarking fatalistically, "The lough will claim a victim every year" and "We'll be the quicker going down."

The second poem, "Beyond Sargasso," picks up the eel's life cycle at the post-larval stage. It is a life cycle dominated by another kind of gravitational pull, for the leptocephalus drifts from the Sargasso Sea across the Atlantic towards Ireland

> sure as the satellite's
> insinuating pull
> in the ocean, as true
> to his orbit.

What reaches the Bann estuary after two years and a further metamorphosis is a transparent elver that has been dubbed a "glass eel," what Heaney calls a "muscled icicle." The glass eel lingers at the river mouth, "hiding by day among gravel, weeds, or mud," but "Dark / delivers him hungering / down each undulation."

Heaney does not re-create the ascent of the elvers up the Bann, so one of the quotations from Day prefixed to the Phoenix edition is appropriate:

At an early period of the summer it is an interesting sight, at the Cutts, near Coleraine, on the same river, to mark the thousands of young Eels there ascending the stream. Hay ropes are suspended over the rocky parts to aid them in overcoming such obstructions. At such places the river is black with the multitudes of young Eels, about three or four inches long, all acting under that mysterious impulse that prompts them to push their course onwards to the lake.

Heaney has digested Day well, for several of the latter's words and phrases from elsewhere in Day's section on the eel—"icicle" and "tidal water"—find their way into the sequence. But, in fact, the particular passage above quoted by Heaney was not written by Day, and I have restored in six instances the grammatical form of the original.

Day uses the version of this passage that occurs in William Thompson's *Natural History of Ireland* (London, 1856), IV. Like Day, Thompson acknowledges the original author of the passage, Robert Patterson, and the passage is to be found in Patterson's *Introduction to Zoology for the Use of Schools* (London, 1849). The anguillous passage of the quotations from Patterson through Thompson and Day to Heaney involves, in the course of a century and a quarter, some considerable metamorphosis *en route*. Thompson's use of Patterson is not, of course, surprising, for these two biologists made free use of each other's notes and observations, being colleagues and successive Presidents of the Natural History and Philosophical Society of Belfast. Patterson edited the fourth volume of Thompson's *Natural History* upon the latter's death. William Thompson (1805–52) and Robert Patterson F.R.S. (1802–72) were leading lights in the intellectually vigorous Belfast of the mid-nineteenth century, contemporaries of Darwin, and two of a long line of distinguished Irish biologists.

The third poem of Heaney's sequence, "Bait," seems in theme and execution something of a filler, though the imagery of darkness continues to be developed, while the imagery of lamplight, leading to the image of eel as taper in the sixth poem, is introduced. Also, the image of the earth as a globe ventilated by worms will recur in the sequence's last poem as the motif of circularity.

"Setting," the fourth poem, evokes the baiting of the hooks and the setting of the lines that sink "out of sight and out of mind / Down to the soft bottom of silt and sand." The "bouquet" of hooks being paid out—cf.

"garland" in "Bait"—goes "back to its true form." Dark descent to origins
is an archetypal, thematic motif in Heaney's poetry. In the last stanza of
"Setting," it is rather heavy-handedly clothed in ritual and spiritual livery
when the accompanying gulls are seen as "responsive acolytes," although
"Not sensible of any *kyrie,* / The fishers, who don't know and never
try, / Pursue the work in hand as destiny."

The destinies of fisherman and eels collide in "Lifting," when the silver eel, grown lough-fat and colorful, is lashed flailing, "a knot of back
and pewter belly," on to the boat, "sucked home like lubrication." A more
natural home is the ocean towards which one autumn the mature eel turns.
In "The Return," the eel seeks her birthplace—her dark origins—swimming out of the lough, down the Bann, and into the north Atlantic, past
Malin Head and Tory island, "a wisp, a wick that is / its own taper and
light / through the weltering dark." Where she was once lost, an orphan,
she lays her eggs and the current carries away slicks of her own discarded,
orphaned spawn.

The life cycle is complete; the fishermen haul in their lines for the
winter. In the sequence's last poem, "Vision," Heaney returns in suitably
circular fashion to superstition, and recalls his own distant and recent experiences. There is a memory of being told that unless he fine-combed his
hair, lice would "gang up / Into a mealy rope / And drag him, small,
dirty, doomed // Down to the water." This accords with the lore that surrounds eels. Mystery has always shrouded these fish, in part because they
behave in odd and even preternatural ways. Thompson records some very
curious happenings, including the way eels once cut off water supplies to
Belfast and plugged a Belfast fireman's hose, while Patterson witnessed a
decapitated conger bite a small boy's foot in Holywood, County Down.
Then there is the corroborated instance of the eels' travelling in autumn
over wet meadows on moonless nights, which provides Heaney with his
concluding conceit and reinforces his darkness imagery. In part, also, the
mystery derives from the genuine ignorance of scientists, even today, about
aspects of the eel's life history. The second quotation from Day prefixed to
the Phoenix edition of Heaney's sequence refers to Aristotle's belief that
eels sprang from mud. In view of this, the worms in "Bait" with their
"mud coronas" might be thought of as eel-like. There is also Helmont's
recipe for making eels out of turves. And, in a passage not quoted by
Heaney, Day remarks upon the Irish folk belief that eels "are the lineal
descendants of the serpents on which St. Patrick served a writ of ejectment,
depriving them of any local habitation on dry land," a writ devilishly
defied by the eels' overland forays. Serpents, worms, eels: all being apodal

and elongated, they serve the purpose of Heaney's final and convolute metaphor.

Fact and fiction, science and folklore are woven by Heaney into Metaphysical conceit in the last stanza of "Vision." The rope of lice—an image perhaps reactivated by Patterson's reference to ropes of hay—is transformed into a cable that, in turn, recalls for the poet the "cable" of eel he recently witnessed traveling across the damp meadow.

> To stand
> In one place as the field flowed
> Past, a jellied road,
> To watch the eels crossing land
>
> Re-wound his world's live girdle.
> Phosphorescent, sinewed slime
> Continued at his feet. Time
> Confirmed the horrid cable.

Perhaps too neatly, the continuity of this eel-cable echoes the continuity of the fishlines, the ropes of lice, and the invisible gravitational "ropes" connecting the eels with their birthplace and the hapless annual fisherman with the deeps of the lough. Circular continuity fulfills the motif of homing. It also fulfills the motif of descent contained in the images of the drowning fisherman, the fishlines, the buried glass eel, the escaping bait-worms, and the spawning eel. The cable winding around the poet's globe of experience recalls for the reader the satellite behavior of the eel in "Beyond Sargasso" in being true to his "Orbit." Orbit implies both fixed, continuous, and global movement, and a contrary and gravitational compulsion to descend, and is arguably—in its ritual and moral implications and tensions—*the* archetypal motif of Heaney's poetry. Lastly, the key actions of the sequence, like the horrid cabling of the eels, takes place in darkness. The flickering lights that illuminate the dark flare up in the picture of the phosphorescent eels sliding like "hatched fears" out of the dark recesses of the poet's psyche and across his consciousness. These fears threaten with ancient, magical, and malign power, yet they curiously lend the poet's world its shape and continuity.

RITA ZOUTENBIER

The Matter of Ireland and the Poetry of Seamus Heaney

Seamus Heaney was born in County Derry, Northern Ireland, in 1939, the oldest of nine children; and spent the first fourteen years of his life at Mossbawn, near Lough Neagh in County Derry, where his father was a farmer and cattle dealer. From the primary school at Anahorish, he moved on to St. Columb's, a Catholic boarding school in Derry, and then to Queen's University, Belfast, where he read English and where, after working in a Belfast secondary school and in a teacher-training college, he returned to teach. In 1972, he gave up teaching for full-time writing, moving with his family to the Irish Republic, to a cottage that was a gate lodge of Glanmore Castle on the former Synge estate in Wicklow. He has since moved back into Dublin, living with his wife and three children in Sandymount, and teaching at Carysfort College, a Catholic teacher-training college, where he is head of the English department. He is a member of the Irish Arts Council, and runs a fortnightly book programme on Irish radio. So far Heaney has published four volumes of poetry, *Death of a Naturalist* (1966), *Door into the Dark* (1969), *Wintering Out* (1972), and *North* (1975); a collection of short autobiographical fragments *Stations* (1975); and a number of critical articles and uncollected poems in different magazines.

Heaney's rural background and the "matter of Ireland" provided him with a subject; his reading of English literature helped to shape his language; or as Heaney has said himself: "I began as a poet when my roots were crossed with my reading." A book by the Danish archeologist, P. V.

From *Dutch Quarterly Review* 9, no. 1 (1979). © 1979 by the *Dutch Quarterly Review*.

Glob, *The Bog People,* which Heaney first read in 1969, became important
to him, when what he found there merged with his own images of bogland, and helped him towards finding symbols and a myth for his own
writing. The reading of the Glob book set off a further interest in archeology, which is apparent in *North:* some of the poems in that volume being
inspired by recent excavations in Ireland. And this interest in archeology
coincides with Heaney's notion of a poem as an archeological find, dug up
from the depths of the memory or imagination.

The fact that Heaney's poetry is so much tied up with a particular
locale may seem a limitation, but his feeling for his own territory is a
source of emotion for the poet, which infuses his language, and makes it
come alive. In a lecture called "The Sense of Place" Heaney has talked
about the "vital and enhancing bond that exists between our consciousness
and our country," and about a "grounding of the self" and an "earthing of
the emotions." In Heaney's later poetry his response to the Irish situation
has become increasingly imaginative and visionary as a "country of the
mind" has replaced the geographical country, though the former is still
rooted in the latter.

One could say that the poetry of Seamus Heaney starts from a sense
of displacement, personal and cultural—Heaney moved away from his
home area, physically as well as in the mind, and has moved away again
from Northern Ireland—which leads to a search for identity and roots
through language; or as Heaney has put it himself, to the making of a
"myth of identity through language." This search starts with the rediscov-
ery and re-creation of Heaney's personal past in *Death of a Naturalist* and
Door into the Dark, volumes which include among other things reminis-
cences of a country childhood. Towards the end of *Door into the Dark* and
in *Wintering Out* Heaney widens his scope to Irish history, and goes deeper
into the origins of his country's culture. The first part of *North* continues
this quest, while the second part deals with day-to-day personal and
political events.

There is a continuous development of theme and style throughout the
four volumes that Heaney has published so far. He has extended his subject
matter from personal memories and private experience to history and mythology and the origins of a culture. The landscape, which features
throughout the poetry, has become associated with history and with language, changing from the actual physical landscape of Heaney's home area,
to a conceptual, cultural landscape embodying the past, or to a visionary
landscape which reveals a kind of sacral history.

Heaney has become more certain of his subject as he has got a closer grip on it with his language: one could characterize his poetry as a continuous attempt to get in touch with a subject or a vision, something that is already there in the imagination but needs to be brought out into the light. Unlike Joyce who uses experience as a starting point from which his language and his imagination take off, Heaney moves inward to his subject. He goes back to the structures which underlie experience, to a life "deeper and older than himself"; and again unlike Joyce he submits himself to his country's history and culture, finding himself through a sense of community rather than in isolation and exile.

DEATH OF A NATURALIST

In "Digging," the opening poem of Heaney's first volume, several items of theme and style that turn out to be characteristic of Heaney's poetry are already evident: the precise observation of physical phenomena (as in the beginning of Joyce's *Portrait* all the five senses play a part); memory which goes back from father to grandfather; a sense of unease and alienation ("But I've no spade to follow men like them"); the search for roots; and the continuation of a tradition (digging with the pen instead of with a spade). The father digging, "nicking and slicing neatly," is the first example of a series of portraits of local craftsmen as a metaphor for the poet: as in "The Diviner," "The Thatcher," and the smith in "The Forge," and others. The "nicking and slicing neatly" corresponds to the craft of the poet shaping his language, while the "going down" and "digging" are another task for the poet, like the plumbing of hidden sources of the diviner. "Making" and "discovering," the "craft" and the "gift" are words which Heaney himself has used several times for these two activities. There are other poems about the writing of poetry in *Death of a Naturalist* and *Door into the Dark*. In "Personal Helicon" Heaney states that the writing of poetry is a search for the self:

> Now, to pry into roots, to finger slime,
> To stare big-eyed Narcissus into some spring
> Is beneath all adult dignity. I rhyme
> To see myself, to set the darkness echoing.

In "The Peninsula" (*Door into the Dark*) poetry is the reshaping of past experience in order to create the self, and to get in touch with the outside world.

The poems in *Death of a Naturalist* can be loosely divided into groups according to theme. The largest group are the poems about childhood, which read like a kind of *Bildungsroman* in verse. They move from a child's

fear in "Death of a Naturalist," and "The Barn" to the conquering of that
fear in "An Advancement of Learning," and the shrugging of shoulders at
the sight of drowning puppies; "Follower" and "Ancestral Photograph" are
about the son succeeding the father. "At a Potato Digging" and "For the
Commander of 'Eliza' " treat a subject from Irish history, the great famine.
"Docker" and "Poor Women in a City Church" present images of the two
cultures in Ireland: the violence of the Belfast docker whose idea of God is
"a foreman with certain definite views / Who orders life in shifts of work
and leisure"; and the submissive women kneeling in a church: "Golden
shrines, altar lace, / Marble columns and cool shadows / Still them." The
volume ends with a group of love poems, and a group of poems about art
and artists such as Synge and Saint Francis who like Heaney derive their
subject from nature.

Death of a Naturalist contains a variety of styles. On the one hand
there is a poem like "Turkeys Observed," a description of slaughtered turkeys in a poultry shop, which is among the earliest poems that Heaney
wrote, a very neat and accurate exercise, very limited in tone and subject
matter. Contrasting with that there is the group of poems about childhood,
where the tone is very personal and open. Most of those poems are written
in free verse. They are the most successful in the volume, where the language gets closest to the experience, even though Heaney lays it on rather
thick at times, for example in the excessive description in the title poem
"Death of a Naturalist." The influence of Hopkins, whom Heaney read as
a student, is noticeable in some of the early poems, in heavily alliterated
lines like "the squelch and slap / Of soggy peat, the curt cuts of an edge."
In "At a Potato Digging" the language imposes a vision on an observed
scene, which does not fit. The potato-diggers are seen as enacting a kind
of pagan ritual, but the religious sentiment expressed does not belong to
them, nor does it belong to Heaney. In a poem like "Waterfall," where a
waterfall is compared to "villains dropped screaming to justice," and the
poet poses as the self-conscious observer: "My eye rides over and downwards, falls with / Hurtling tons that slabber and spill", the language becomes too fanciful in its metaphors and diverts attention from the object
described. Heaney is at his best in this volume when he describes his own
personal experience, and he has not much grip yet on a subject that lies
outside himself, like history or inanimate nature.

DOOR INTO THE DARK

The poems in Door into the Dark are linked not so much by a theme as by a common mood or metaphor. Darkness in one form or another occurs in most of the poems and embodies different though not unconnected things. In the title poem it dramatizes the poet's uncertainty: "All I know is a door into the dark." In this volume Heaney is groping about in the dark, trying to get a grasp on his subject. In a poem like "The Forge" he is not very successful. The smith, like Kelly's bull in "The Outlaw," retires into the dark, as if he ultimately escaped the poet. In the first three poems of the volume, "Night-Piece," "Gone," and "Dream," the subjects seem to come up out of the dark of the imagination, but they remain half-hidden there. In "The Peninsula" and in "In Gallarus Oratory" the dark is the place where one needs to retire in order to achieve a vision. This vision is not something that lies outside the common order of things but an illumination or heightening of the ordinary: "things founded clear on their own shapes," "the sea a censer, and the grass a flame," like the renewal of the "smells of ordinariness" in "Night Drive." In the latter poem the movement is the same as in the other two: traveling, immersion in the dark, and coming back with a vision. There are sexual undertones, but they escape analysis. These poems are as much about how to live, as how to write or to make art. For both it is necessary to establish an intimate contact with the outside world. In "In Gallarus Oratory" this amounts to the erotic visions of the mystic; but the poem is about that kind of vision or writing, it is not itself an embodiment of it, as are some later poems of Heaney's. "The Plantation" is another poem about the problem of living and/or writing. Losing oneself without being lost, "following whim deliberately" ("The Return"), to be in control while at the same time surrendering oneself, are necessary conditions. "A line goes out of sight and out of mind / Down to the soft bottom of silt and sand / Past the indifferent skill of the hunting hand" ("Setting"), is another metaphor for the writing of poetry. In "A Lough Neagh Sequence," a poem about the life cycle of eels, the dark has a more explicitly sexual meaning in the life of the eels, as well as cosmic significance. It is a poem full of circular movements, dramatizing this cycle and the "horrid cable" in which both human and animal are caught without distinction. The sequence ends in fear (a more adult version of the fear in *Death of a Naturalist*) of the dark cosmic processes for which there is no resolution.

The latter part of *Door into the Dark* contains a few poems which point forward to further developments. "Relic of Memory" is the first poem about relics in the bog and the attraction they have for the poet. "Shoreline" is about the ritual timeless moment which brings the poet into contact with sacral history, which is revealed in the landscape:

> Listen. Is it the Danes,
> A black hawk bent on the sail?
> Or the chinking Normans?
> Or currachs hopping high
>
> Or to the sand?

"Bogland," at the end of the volume, is the first poem where the bog becomes a mythical landscape and a symbol for Ireland:

> Melting and opening underfoot,
> Missing its last definition
> By millions of years.
> They'll never dig coal here,
>
> Only the waterlogged trunks
> Of great firs, soft as pulp.
> Our pioneers keep striking
> Inwards and downwards,
>
> Every layer they strip
> Seems camped on before.
> The bogholes might be Atlantic seepage.
> The wet centre is bottomless.

WINTERING OUT

In *Door into the Dark* Heaney had already extended his scope beyond the strictly personal; in *Wintering Out* he goes further in this direction, though he approaches his subject matter in a rather cautious and hesitant manner at first. The five poems with which the volume opens are about the Irish colonial past, but this is only indicated through allusions. The mood in the poems is desolate, there is a sense of starvation and of the shrinking of life, but one does not know why. They are not located specifically in time or place. "These long nights," "those mound-dwellers," "the back end of a bad year," "some outhouse," could be any time and any place. The poet's vision is blurred by fog and rain ("mizzling rain / blurs the far end / of the cart track," "Those mound-dwellers / go waist-deep in mist") and he is hesitant to approach or accept it. He is merely pondering a possibility: "I might tarry / with the moustached / dead," "Perhaps I just make out / Edmund Spenser." The poem "Bog Oak" presents a rather sharp contrast between the English and native experience:

> Edmund Spenser,
> dreaming sunlight,
> encroached upon by
>
> geniuses who creep
> "out of every corner
> of the woodes and glennes"
> towards watercress and carrion.

Edmund Spenser's pastoral vision is not for Ireland, but these poems are not entirely desolate. "The Last Mummer" ends with hope and the possibility of a new beginning. "Anahorish" (meaning "place of clear water") is a version of Gaelic pastoral or the poet's personal Helicon, which first fertilized his imagination. It is the first poem where landscape becomes language: "soft gradient / of consonant, vowel meadow."

"Land," "Gifts of Rain," and "Oracle" present the poet in a relationship of close intimacy with the land. In "Gifts of Rain" he states what this intimacy means to him as a poet:

> I cock my ear
> at an absence—
> in the shared calling of blood
>
> arrives my need
> for antediluvian lore.
> Soft voices of the dead
> are whispering by the shore
>
> that I would question
> (and for my children's sake)
> about crops rotted, river mud
> glazing the baked clay floor.

The function of poetry is no longer private: the shaping of one's own identity. But the poet assigns himself a public role:

> a mating call of sound
> rises to pleasure me, Dives,
> hoarder of common ground.

The next series of poems are about language and landscape and the two cultural and language traditions in Ireland. "Toome," like "Broagh" and "Anahorish" is a place-name poem (the writing of poems explaining the names of places is an old genre in Irish literature). Here the sound of the

Gaelic words "anahorish," "broagh," and "Toome" (all names connected
with Heaney's home area), draw the poet back into the past of the land and
the language. These poems, like "A New Song," are an attempt to incorporate and combine both the Gaelic and the English tradition. Heaney himself, in an interview with Seamus Deane, has said about these poems: "I
had a great sense of release as they were being written, a joy and devil-may-
careness, and that convinced me that one could be faithful to the nature of
the English language—for in some senses these poems are erotic mouth-
music by and out of the Anglo-Saxon tongue—and, at the same time, be
faithful to one's own non-English origin, for me that is County Derry." "A
New Song" is a rallying poem, written out of impatience with the state of
cultural affairs, the separateness of the two cultures:

> But now our river tongues must rise
> From licking deep in native haunts
> To flood, with vowelling embrace,
> Demesnes staked out in consonants.
>
> And Castledawson we'll enlist
> And Upperlands, each planted bawn—
> Like bleaching-greens resumed by grass—
> A vocable, as rath and ballaun.

Words like "demesne," "Castledawson," "Upperlands," "bawn," "bleach-
ing-greens" call up the English colonization of Ireland. In "The Trade of
an Irish Poet" Heaney has said: "I think of the personal and Irish pieties
as vowels, and the literary awarenesses nourished on English as consonants.
My hope is that the poems will be vocables adequate to my whole
experience."

"Linen Town," the poem that precedes the sequence "A Northern
Hoard," is about the irreversibility of history. "A Northern Hoard," like
the introductory poem of *Wintering Out* about an internment camp, treats
the present violent situation in Northern Ireland in language that refers to
the actual situation (words like "gunshot," "siren" and "clucking gas," and
"sniper") but also puts it in a mythological perspective. "Roots," the first
poem of the sequence is about the "nightmare of history" intruding into
people's private lives, and the failure of ordinary human feelings like love,
in that situation. In "No Man's Land" there is a sense of guilt at the inade-
quacy of one's reaction. "Stump" is about the failure of poetry: "What do
I say if they wheel out their dead? / I'm cauterized, a black stump of
home." In "No Sanctuary" and "Tinder" there is a sense of complicity

within a community. In "Tinder" "cold beads of history and home," relics of the past, fail to light up the imagination: "What could strike a blaze / From our dead igneous days?" The present violent situation cuts one off from a sense of continuity with the past: "new history, flint and iron / Cast-off, scraps, nail, canine." The poems are full of images of pagan rituals and animal savagery and have an almost surrealist quality:

> Leaf membranes lid the window.
> In the streetlamp's glow
> Your body's moonstruck
> To drifted barrow, sunk glacial rock.
>
> And all shifts dreamily as you keen
> Far off, turning from the din
> Of gunshot, siren and clucking gas
> Out there beyond each curtained terrace
>
> Where the fault is opening. The touch of love
> Your warmth heaving to the first move,
> Grows helpless in our old Gomorrah.
> We petrify or uproot now.

"The Tollund Man" is the first of a series of poems about bog people which Heaney wrote after reading P. V. Glob's *The Bog People*. The poems of "A Northern Hoard" can be said to be public poems in so far as they deal with communal experience. In "The Tollund Man" Heaney goes on a private imaginary pilgrimage to Denmark: "Some day I will go to Aarhus"; but he hesitates to commit himself fully to this pagan religion: "I could risk blasphemy / Consecrate the cauldron bog / Our holy ground." The poem ends in speculation:

> Something of his sad freedom
> As he rode the tumbril
> Should come to me, driving,
> Saying the names
>
> Tollund, Grabaulle, Nebelgard,
> Watching the pointing hands
> Of country people,
> Not knowing their tongue.
>
> Out there in Jutland
> In the old man-killing parishes

> I will feel lost,
> Unhappy and at home.

The first section of *Wintering Out* ends with a few poems which recall again scenes from Heaney's home area, but there is a felt distance now:

> What can fend us now
> Can soothe the hurt eye
> Of the sun,
> Unpoison great lakes,
> Turn back
> The rat on the road.

If one takes the introductory poem of *Wintering Out* as the context for the whole volume, then the poems of the second part seem a retreat into a private world of marriage and home, or to stand for the continuity of ordinary human life in the context of violence. Of the marriage poems the best is "Summer Home," about guilt and complicity in a private relationship. The form of the poem is much freer than that of the rest of the poems in the volume: and the breaking off of the lines in the middle of a sentence after a stressed syllable creates the tension the poem is about.

Apart from the marriage poems there is a group of poems about Irish folktales written in a dramatic narrative style reminiscent of Robert Frost—who influenced Heaney to some degree—especially the poem "Shore-woman." In "First Calf" Heaney projects his own changed sensibility and the pain of existence into a recalled scene, whereas the poem "May" presents a picture of original innocence and peace. In the final poem in the volume "Westering" Heaney takes his distance from Ireland:

> Six thousand miles away,
> I imagine untroubled dust,
> A loosening gravity,
> Christ weighing by his hands.

NORTH

Whereas the introductory poem of *Wintering Out* puts the volume into a context of violence, the two introductory poems of *North* put in it in a framework of peacefulness and permanence. "Sunlight" is a very clear and tranquil vision of a domestic scene; and in "The Seedcutters" a pastoral scene which lies fixed in history outside time, is embodied in a very balanced poem. The poem expresses a desire for permanence:

O calendar customs! Under the broom
Yellowing over them, compose the frieze
With all of us there, our anonymities.

The volume *North* itself is divided into two contasting sections. Heaney told Seamus Deane "the two halves of the book constitute two different types of utterance, each of which arose out of a necessity to shape and give palpable linguistic form to two kinds of urgency—one symbolic, one explicit." Yeats and Kavanagh represent these two poles in poetry, they "point up the contradictions we have been talking about: the search for myths and sagas, the need for a structure and a sustaining landscape and at the same time the need to be liberated and distanced from it, the need to be open, unpredictably susceptible, lyrically opportunistic."

The first section of *North* begins and ends with two not very successful allegorical poems "Antaeus" and "Hercules and Antaeus." Antaeus is an image of the instinctive poet who derives his strength from the earth and whose "elevation" or education is his "fall." The application of the allegory in the context of the volume is not very clear.

"Belderg" is a poem about an excavation done in Mayo. The "quern-stones out of a bog" connect the imagination with the past:

To lift the lid of the peat
And find this pupil dreaming
Of neolithic wheat!
When he stripped off blanket bog
The soft-piled centuries

Fell open like a glib:
There were the first plough-marks,
The stone-age fields, the tomb
Corbelled, turfed and chambered,
Floored with dry turf-coomb.

A landscape fossilized,
Its stone-wall patternings
Repeated before our eyes
In the stone walls of Mayo.

The discussion about the word "Mossbawn" (the name of Heaney's birthplace), which is seen to contain Irish, Norse, and English roots and therefore presents the mixed cultural heritage of Ireland, is resolved by the poet, who passes "through the eye of the quern," in a test of the imagination, and sees "A worldtree of balanced stones, / Querns piled like vertebrae, / The marrow crushed to grounds"—an image of a mixed culture.

"Funeral Rites" is again (like "A Northern Hoard") a poem which combines the actual with the mythological. In the first part the poet sees himself as a member of a culture in which the dead are buried with elaborate ritual. There is a detailed description of the dead, as in the poems about bog corpses, in a volume where Heaney is preoccupied with fossils, bones, skeletons, corpses. In the second and third parts the poet imagines the reinstitution of ritual, which involves the whole country in a gigantic funeral procession, to cope with the present situation in Ireland, in which murder is a frequent occurrence.

In "North," as in the poem "Shoreline" in *Door into the Dark*, there is a shift from the secular to the sacral, and the poet is almost overwhelmed by a vision of Viking raids in Ireland, of which the present situation is a continuation ("memory incubating the spilled blood"). But he is told to retain his power of vision and to go on writing:

> It said, 'Lie down
> in the word-hoard, burrow
> the coil and the gleam
> of your furrowed brain.
>
> Compose in darkness.
> Expect aurora borealis
> in the long foray
> but no cascade of light.
>
> Keep your eye clear
> as the bleb of the icicle,
> trust the feel of what nubbed treasure
> your hands have known.'

The poem "Viking Dublin: Trial Pieces" is one long flowing line of associations, starting at the sight of a piece of incised bone exhibited in the National Museum in Dublin, and involving history and art and death, in language that implies a gay acceptance:

> 'Did you ever hear tell,'
> said Jimmy Farrell,
> 'of the skulls they have
> in the city of Dublin?

> White skulls and black skulls
> and yellow skulls, and some
> with full teeth, and some
> haven't only but one,'

In "Bone Dreams," as in the poem "Toome" in *Wintering Out*, the poet goes back to origins which lie beyond language:

> Come back past
> philology and kennings,
> re-enter memory
> where the bone's lair
>
> is a love-nest
> in the grass.
> I hold my lady's head
> like a crystal
>
> and ossify myself
> by gazing: I am screes
> on her escarpments,
> a chalk giant
>
> carved upon her downs.
> Soon my hands, on the sunken
> fosse of her spine
> move towards the passes.

In "Funeral Rites" Heaney imagined a community and a ritual for the community; in the series of poems about bog corpses he turns to communion with the landscape, and what is concealed there, in private meditation, in order to come to terms with the violence in Ireland. The tone of these poems is much more assured than in "The Tollund Man" in *Wintering Out*. Heaney has now found a focus for his imagination, a myth which encompasses past and present. The intimate communing with these preserved bodies leads to an almost complete identification:

> I can feel the tug
> of the halter at the nape
> of her neck, the wind
> on her naked front.

But in the same poem ("Punishment") Heaney admits to an ambiguity of feeling:

> I almost love you
> but would have cast, I know,
> the stones of silence.
> I am the artful voyeur
>
> of your brain's exposed
> and darkened combs,
> your muscles' webbing
> and all your numbered bones:
>
> I who have stood dumb
> when your betraying sisters,
> cauled in tar,
> wept by the railings,
>
> who could connive
> in civilized outrage
> yet understand the exact
> and tribal, intimate revenge.

Though these poems contain references to the present situation in Ireland, they can also be read as poems about the universal fate of man:

> As if he had been poured
> in tar, he lies
> on a pillow of turf
> and seems to weep
>
> the black river of himself.

The bog is not only a symbol for Ireland as a female goddess to whom sacrifices are made but also the "all-tombing womb" of the earth mother where the bog corpses lie buried like embryos awaiting rebirth. These poems may express an unwillingness on Heaney's part to come to terms with the situation in Northern Ireland in more direct terms, but they may equally stem from a private need to come to terms with universals. The poem "Kinship" is a kind of finale which gathers up the images of the bog that have occurred in Heaney's poetry. It contains references to earlier poems, and there is a kind of ritual summing up:

> Earth-pantry, bone-vault,
> sun-bank, embalmer
> of votive goods
> and sabred fugitives.

> Insatiable bride.
> Sword-swallower,
> casket, midden,
> floe of history.
>
> Ground that will strip
> its dark side,
> nesting ground,
> outback of my mind.

Walking down the bog the poet walks back in time and stands "at the edge of centuries / facing a goddess"—the earth goddess of Irish history and of time. In the poem "Bogland" in *Door into the Dark* the "wet centre" of the bog was "bottomless." Here the centre has gathered meaning, and "holds and spreads"; it has revealed the congruence between present and past, and given an image of the country's cultural identity. The poet accepts being tied to this ground, which means an acceptance of the culture of which he is a member, and of history and fate:

> I grew out of all this
> like a weeping willow
> inclined to
> the appetites of gravity.

In the second part of *North* Heaney turns from Norse mythology to the actual North of Ireland and a more public kind of poetry:

> I'm writing just after an encounter
> With an English journalist in search of 'views
> On the Irish thing'.

The style has changed from the heightened to the satiric and the debunking, with stanzas rhyming a-b-a-b:

> Yet I live here, I live here too, I sing,
>
> Expertly civil tongued with civil neighbours
> On the high wires of first wireless reports,
> Sucking the fake taste, the stony flavours
> Of those sanctioned, old, elaborate retorts:
>
> "Oh, it's disgraceful, surely, I agree,"
> "Where's it going to end?" "It's getting worse."
> "They're murderers." "Internment, understandably . . ."
>
> The "voice of sanity" is getting hoarse.

"Whatever You Say Say Nothing" is like "The Other Side" in *Wintering Out*, about rituals of coexistence between the two communities, which imply submitting to a code:

> "Religion's never mentioned here," of course.
> "You know them by their eyes," and hold your tongue.
> "One side's as bad as the other," never worse.
> Christ, it's near time that some small leak was sprung
>
> In the great dykes the Dutchman made
> To dam the dangerous tide that followed Seamus.
> Yet for all this art and sedentary trade
> I am incapable. The famous
>
> Northern reticence, the tight gag of place
> And times: yes, yes. Of the "wee six" I sing
> Where to be saved you only must save face
> And whatever you say, you say nothing.

It is also a poem about different kinds of language: the language of codes of the community, the clichés of journalism ("escalate", backlash", "crackdown") and the language of poetry, all inadequate to cope with the situation:

> (It's tempting here to rhyme on "labour pangs"
> And diagnose a rebirth in our plight
> But that would be to ignore other symptoms.
> Last night you didn't need a stethoscope
> To hear the eructation of Orange drums
> Allergic equally to Pearse and Pope.)
>
> On all sides "little platoons" are mustering—
> The phrase is Cruise O'Brien's via that great
> Backlash, Burke—while I sit here with a pestering
> Drouth for words at once both gaff and bait
>
> To lure the tribal shoals to epigram
> An order. I believe any of us
> Could draw the line through bigotry and sham
> Given the right line, *aere perennius*.

"Freedman" is about the poet's emancipation from submission to religion and society, and yet another kind of language ("Memento homo quia pulvis es") to the freedom that poetry has given him. It precedes the sequence

"Singing School" where Heaney returns to autobiographical material but in a very different way than in *Death of a Naturalist*. The landscape is now peopled by policemen and Orangemen instead of local characters. The quotation from Wordsworth "Fair seedtime had my soul, and I grew up / Fostered alike by beauty and by fear" gets another poignant meaning in a Northern Irish context, where one's name assigns one to one side of the community and where a representative of the law, or the threatening sound of Orange drums, inspire one with fear. "Summer 1969" (a summer in which trouble broke out in Belfast) is again about the need for myth or art to come to terms with present happenings. At a remove from the actual situations, watching television during a holiday in Spain, and hearing the news from home, the poet retreats to the Prado to look at "Shootings of the Third of May," a painting by Goya, which is a more real representation of violence than the impersonal "real thing" on television. According to this poem the only possible commitment is through art, though it also suggests the other possibility:

> "Go back," one said, "try to touch the people."
> Another conjured Lorca from his hill.

In the next poem "Exposure," the last in the volume, neither possibility offers solace. The poet is removed from his people—unlike in the first poem of the second part, "The Unacknowledged Legislator's Dream," where the poet sees himself in a dream at the centre of his community, and poetry has also lost its meaning:

> How did I end up like this?
> I often think of my friends'
> Beautiful prismatic counselling
> And the anvil brains of some who hate me
>
> As I sit weighing and weighing
> My responsible *tristia*.
> For what? For the ear? For the people?
> For what is said behind-backs?
>
> Rain comes down through the alders,
> Its low conducive voices
> Mutter about let-downs and erosions
> And yet each drop recalls
>
> The diamond absolutes.
> I am neither internee nor informer;

An inner émigré, grown long-haired
And thoughtful; a wood-kerne

Escaped from the massacre,
Taking protective colouring
From bole and bark, feeling
Every wind that blows;

Who, blowing up these sparks
For their meagre heat, have missed
The once-in-a-lifetime portent,
The comet's pulsing rose.

This seems like an ending but more likely points to a different direction in Heaney's development. He has talked about this in an interview with Monie Begley:

> The book ends up in Wicklow in December '73. It's in some ways the book all books were leading to. You end up with nothing but your vocation, with words and your own free choice. Isolated but not dispossessed of what produced you. Having left a context, stepped away, you can't really go back. It ends up with just the responsibility of the artist, whatever that is, and that responsibility has no solutions.
>
> I would say that I am a product of that isolation we were talking about before. And for me now it's just the usual middle-age coasting toward extinction, but trying to define the self. I'm not interested in my poetry canvassing public events deliberately any more. I would like to write poems of myself at this age. Poems, so far, have been fueled by a world that is gone or a world that is too much with us—public events. Just through accident and all the things we've been talking about, I've ended up with myself, and I have to start there, you know.

P. R. KING

"I Step through Origins"

THE DIGNITY OF SIMPLICITIES

Seamus Heaney began publishing his first poems in the early 1960s and is the oldest of a group of Ulster poets who have produced consistently interesting and valuable poems over the last ten years.

The rural landscape of Heaney's childhood forms the background to many of his poems and is frequently the central subject of the best. His work often reminds us that until recently Ireland has been the only country in northern Europe to retain something approaching a genuinely peasant culture, and the traditions and rituals of that culture, together with the spirit of Ireland's rural history, emerge in many of Heaney's poems. This spirit is related to his own childhood and early family memories. His first book, *Death of a Naturalist,* was published in 1966 and has been followed by *Door into the Dark* (1969), *Wintering Out* (1972), *North* (1975), and *Field Work* (1979). These titles alone speak of his subjects: nature, the seasons, the countryside and its community, a sense of the past and the dark undercurrent of danger and menace in Irish life, both in past centuries and in the present political instability.

Heaney has proved to be popular with the poetry-reading public, often having an immediate appeal because of his accurate descriptive powers and the clarity of his figurative language. The following lines exemplify his immediacy:

> Clouds ran their wet mortar, plastered the daybreak
> Grey. The stones clicked tartly
> If we missed the sleepers but mostly

From *Nine Contemporary Poets: A Critical Introduction.* © 1979 by P. R. King. Methuen, 1979. Originally entitled " 'I step through origins' The Poetry of Seamus Heaney."

Silent we headed up the railway
Where now the only steam was funnelling from cows
Ditched on their rumps beyond hedges,
Cudding, watching, and knowing.

("Dawn Shoot")

The superficial clarity of this poetry, especially in his first two volumes, is something that has aroused disagreement among Heaney's critics and reviewers. All reviewers of *Death of a Naturalist* praised the way the poet created a sense of this rural Irish life, but a difference of opinion arose over the value of such descriptions. Writing in the *Kenyon Review,* David Galler spent a considerable proportion of his review pursuing an argument that sought to make a distinction between descriptive poetry which remains "exposition" and descriptive poetry with "complication." He maintained that description-exposition poems are merely the attempt to give reality to what is described, whereas description-complication poems occur when the poet uses his observation not just to re-create a scene but also to impart a universal significance to the individual particulars of that description. Galler argues that the latter type of poetry (exemplified in Wordsworth) has most lasting value and that Heaney does not achieve this kind of poem. Apart from ignoring the fact that a young poet might be forgiven for not yet writing at the level of the mature Wordsworth, Galler comes close to confusing surface clarity of expression in poetry with banality of theme and ideas. He underestimates Heaney's capacity to breathe a universal significance into his best descriptions (in "Blackberry-Picking," for example). What Heaney is not doing is setting out to write poems of ideas as such. The source of many of his best poems is a memory of childhood experiences which he then renders accurately and almost physically in a direct language that shuns obscurity of expression. This may be a virtue often underestimated among literary academics and reviewers but which, nevertheless, gives Heaney's work a powerful precision and lucidity.

Death of a Naturalist includes many poems that have the countryside or animals as their subject, and yet it would be a mistake to see Heaney as a nature poet. It is the country experiences, the community and its traditions, the craftsmen and the village rituals that most interest the poet, and his deeper themes are concerned with growing up and maturing in such a rural life. This early volume contains three groups of poems: those directly concerned with his rural childhood, those that re-create the physical presence of animals (usually connected with childhood experiences as well) and a small group of love poems.

It is the first group that provides the more important poems, but a prior comment on the other two groups might be helpful. The poems about animals develop from the poet's boyhood memories of farm life. The animals are domestic (turkeys and cows) or those encountered on hunting or fishing expeditions (like trout); they are not the wild, untamed animals that fill the early poems of Ted Hughes, but Heaney does share some of Hughes's ability to describe an animal with great accuracy and liveliness. Yet Heaney's descriptions are made as from an observer's point of view: he does not try to re-create the presence of the animal from within the animal as Hughes does. It is usually the effect upon the poet-child-observer that is dwelt upon (see "Turkeys Observed").

The love poems are light and witty, frequently built upon a simple extended metaphor and offering a warm, sunny glimpse of an uncomplicated love. In them even the parting of the lovers cannot be seen as disastrous or final:

> In your presence
> Time rode easy, anchored
> On a smile, but absence
> Rocked love's balance, unmoored
> The days. . . .
> Until you resume command
> Self is in mutiny.
>
> ("Valediction")

But the mutiny seems a mild affair, a matter of wit rather than passion, and we have no doubt that she will resume command. Probably the best of these rather delicate poems is "Honeymoon Flight" which gives us a sense of the lovers' tentatively built trust in their newly married state. This is created though a description of the flight of the aeroplane as it carries them off to their honeymoon. As it flies through turbulence the passengers feel safe only because they trust the crew, and this is used as an image of the trust the lovers have placed in marriage. This simple idea is made effective by the quality of the description of the flight itself, its accuracy and its tone. "The coastline slips away beneath the wing-tip" and

> Below, the patchwork earth, dark hems of hedge,
> The long grey tapes of road that bind and loose
> Villages and fields in casual marriage:

This suggests a connection between the marriage of landscape and community and the lovers themselves. The countryside's patchwork pattern is

stitched into the garment of the landscape and drawn together by the "grey
tapes of roads." The word "casual" implies a relationship that is easy and
natural and suggests the lovers' trust in a marriage which has been
launched into a flight that will reveal the pattern of their lives. The tone
is tender, the theme and language clear and straightforward. A basically
iambic rhythm nevertheless allows secondary stresses on the adjectives in
"dark hems" and "long grey tapes," and has the effect of slowing down the
run of the first two lines so helping create the impression of the slowly
turning landscape (suggested, too, by the accumulation of long vowel
sounds), thus undermining a too stolid rhythm which would have marred
the tentative step of the central idea of trust.

The virtues of a simple originality of image and diction can be seen
more clearly in the poems about childhood and rural life. Two of the best
of these are "Churning Day" and "Blackberry-Picking." "Churning Day"
captures the ancient ritual of farm life in the days before mechanization in
its description of the hand churning of milk into butter. It is built on a
traditional iambic norm which holds in the details, binding together a
strong percussive diction that creates a pressure against the steady but
forceful flow of plosives. Adjectives and adverbs cluster thickly, and this
concatenation in the diction suggests the noise and hard work of the opera-
tion. This roughness also avoids any suggestion that the poet is writing a
"Country Life" idyll. His intention is twofold: to give a feeling of the hard
physical slog of butter making, and to re-create a boy's sensuous observations. It was through his eyes and ears that the boy watched. For him
churning day means not so much the end product of butter but the noise,
energy, and bustle of the activity itself. From the opening onwards the
poem is alive with this energy:

> A thick crust, coarse-grained as limestone rough-cast,
> hardened gradually on top of the four crocks
> that stood, large pottery bombs, in the small pantry.

The choice of "pottery bombs" may be an intrusive feature, but otherwise
the "k" sounds and the limestone simile perfectly bring out the quality of
a crust on standing milk. As the poem develops it concentrates its energy
increasingly into the verbs ("scoured," "spilled," "plunged," "spattered,"
etc.), building up a flurry of noise and activity and of the skilled work of
the mother, until by the end (in a phrase embodying the tiring slog of it
all) she,

> set up rhythms
> that slugged and thumped for hours. Arms ached.
> Hands blistered.

This may be a delightful world for the grown man's memory to be drawn back into, but for those who lived in it then it was a tough, unceasing life of labour, and Heaney preserves the endurance of the people in the strength of his sounds and rhythms.

The core of the poem, buried within the imitative sounds and rhythms of the day's work, is the theme of the process of purification and transformation. It is not a meditative or contemplative poem and, since Heaney, as pointed out earlier, is not primarily a poet of ideas, this theme is not worked out as a concept. It does not perhaps achieve the full generalizing power that Mr. Galler thinks necessary for the greatest descriptive poetry. But what Heaney does do is to look hard and closely at the ritual and seize the sense of it for the child who plays in the middle of it on the "flagged kitchen floor." It is therefore an idea of *the senses*, not of the mind, and suggests that the churning is perhaps a process of purification whose effect on the boy and the young man remembering his past is implied but not stated. We experience this idea through the child's eyes and ears and it is the accumulation of sensuous detail that matters: the crocks "spilled their heavy lip / of cream, their white insides, into the sterile churn." The child *feels* more than thinks of the patient process as the mother works on to the limits of her aching arms and blistered hands so that "finally gold flecks / began to dance" until in a final, sudden moment "a yellow curd was weighting the churned up white." It is not a fanciful poetic image to describe the final butter as "coagulated sunlight," for the young boy must have seen this as a magic act, a mother's Midas touch, and the startling gold yellow of the butter was a regular miracle for the child. Thus earlier in the poem it is the child's sense of strange power that allows the poet to describe the cow's initial transformation of grass into milk as "the hot brewery of gland, cud and udder" and the house after churning as stinking "acrid as a sulphur mine." Although requiring an adult's knowledge, these images are demanded by the remembered *child's* sensuous response. And thus each constituent of the poem underlines the physical and emotional experience, including movement and sound being picked out in this description:

> And in the house we moved with gravid ease,
> our brains turned crystals full of clean deal churns,
> the plash and gurgle of the sour-breathed milk,
> the pat and slap of small spades on wet lumps.

Mr. Galler sees this poem as no more than an accumulation of descriptive details. This is too dismissive and does not take account of the fact that the act of description is valuable in itself when it helps us to see plainly and feel deeply the experience at its heart. His damning of phrases like "hot brewery of gland," "busy scrubber," "churning day," and "purified" for being "phrases with mysterious implications" but no depth overlooks the obvious point that each is an altogether accurate description of part of the activity and what mystery the poet sees in them is only an "implication" for the young boy. Christopher Ricks's comment in an early review is far more justified: "What is surprising is the dignity with which Mr. Heaney invests such simplicities, such as 'wet lumps'."

In "Blackberry-Picking" we have a similar approach to a familiar childhood ritual. Utilizing the same basic rhythm (although with frequent inversions of stress that move it away from the iambic norm of the two poems), Heaney this time employs greater use of rhyme, particularly assonance and half-rhyme. There is again the attempt to re-create a physical sense of the activity, and he stresses the appeal of the fruit in its various stages to eye, hand, and tongue:

> At first, just one, a glossy purple clot
> Among others, red, green, hard as a knot.
> You ate that first one and its flesh was sweet
> Like thickened wine:

But in this poem there is a more conscious attempt to see and place the childhood experience through the conceptualizing of the adult:

> Like thickened wine: summer's blood was in it
> Leaving stains upon the tongue and lust for
> Picking.

"Blood" and "lust" might seem to be overdoing it, perhaps falsely exaggerating the particulars to create a universal significance, yet the trail of the pickers is smeared throughout with suggestions of blood, appropriately both creating a sense of the overpowering desire for the fruit (which makes the pickers endure the most precarious positions and painful lacerations), and also preparing for the second part of the poem in which the failed attempt to store the fruit modulates into the child's first awareness of the experience of disillusion. Precisely because this idea arises naturally from the description, we feel in the end no overworked attempt to moralize. The final line both contains an accurate recall of childhood and raises the subject towards a full-bodied image of our natural human inclination to hang on to what has given us great pleasure. Linked, as it is, to the seasons' cycle ("summer's blood was in it") and hinting at the unbridled nature of our first gluttony for the fruit (berries at the top of the can are "big dark blobs [which] burned / Like a plate of eyes" observing and yet attracting the greed), we are prepared for the terms of the final disillusion:

> Once off the bush
> The fruit fermented, the sweet flesh would turn sour.
> I always felt like crying. It wasn't fair
> That all the lovely canfuls smelt of rot.
> Each year I hoped they'd keep, knew they would not.

That last straightforward comment on the yearly experience brings the poem to a sharp halt with its final return to the everyday reality, eschewing any portentous symbols yet allowing a wider meaning to arise naturally from the child's experience. The possible moral is there because it *is* part of the growing awareness of this country child. Reality relentlessly tempers his dreams—a theme central to both the first two books.

GROWING UP

Maturity and the experiences of childhood that hurry it forth are at the heart of several of the finest poems in the early books. The title poem of the first volume and "An Advancement of Learning" are two very successful evocations of moments of growing up.

"Death of a Naturalist" shares many of the characteristics of the poems already examined. A childhood experience is again conveyed in a vigorous diction, this time riding on a four-/five-stress line which only approximates to an iambic norm.

> All the year the flax-dam festered in the heart
> Of the townland; green and heavy headed
> Flax had rotted there, weighted down by huge sods.
> Daily it sweltered in the punishing sun.

An extra syllable in the third line is used to slow down the speed of the rhythm, pulling down its centre of gravity, as it were, and using the caesura of the second line to separate the generalized opening from the particulars following. This prepares "festered in the heart" (which is emphasized by taking the stress at the end of the line) as a prelude to the theme of the whole poem. That theme is developed tangentially through the evocation of the experience and not by direct comment, according to the procedure of the poems already looked at.

In the first half of the poem the boy collects tadpoles among the flax-dam in order to carry them home to observe "The fattening dots burst into nimble- / Swimming tadpoles." His teacher would tell him of the "daddy" frog and how it was called "a bullfrog" and "how the mammy frog / Laid hundreds of little eggs." It was cosy, domestic, clear, and lovely. The frogs were outside him, collected, observed, controlled by him and even used for predicting the weather:

> You could tell the weather by frogs too
> For they were yellow in the sun and brown
> In rain.

But in the second half of the poem comes the decisive experience of "one hot day when fields were rank / With cowdung" ("rank" and the excretory image indicate the change of tone), and he comes across hundreds of frogs croaking loudly in the flax-dam. They look obscene and threatening and he runs from them, for he sees them as an invading enemy shouting at him in anger. The familiar isolated calls he has heard before suddenly become a huge chorus of "coarse croaking." He is utterly revolted by their pulsing life and their apparent abandonment of their previously tame existence. They have become "great slime kings," no longer tame or domestic or controlled, and he can no longer maintain a detached view. They insist on reminding him that they have a life of their own and one that is unrelievedly physical. The last image of the poem—". . . and I knew / That if I dipped my hand the spawn would clutch it"—shows how the boy's attitude has changed. The frogs are now on the offensive and control the boy. No explicit statement explores the theme, but the presentation of this total image of the experience leaves us in no doubt of the physical quality of a moment when the boy suddenly realizes his youth is turning into manhood. Leaving behind a state of nature, a feeling of at-homeness with natural processes, the language of the second half of the poem is used to create the sense of distaste and fear for the physicality and sexuality of adolescence that the boy is beginning to feel. The description of the frogs shows this clearly enough (I have italicized the words carrying a submerged sexual association):

> The air was thick with a *bass* chorus.
> Right down the dam *gross-bellied* frogs were *cocked*
> On sods; their loose necks *pulsed* like sails. Some hopped:
> The slap and pop were *obscene threats.* Some sat
> Poised like mud grenades, their *blunt* heads *farting.*

The boy's revulsion at his own sexuality, the young adolescent's smutty embarrassment at his body, are projected on to the frogs. In these lines description blends perfectly with "complication" to create a generalizable theme without over-exploiting the particulars of the description. This poem is a perfect fusion of description and comment in a single experience. The title is given to the whole volume in which the poem appears because the predominant theme of that book is growing up. The community described in the poems may be particular, but the experience of maturation is a universal one.

"An Advancement of Learning" takes even further the idea of the menace in an experience of the repulsive side of nature and uses it to reveal the growing power of the maturity in the boy. This is the experience of a slightly older adolescent. While walking along the river embankment, he encounters two rats and recalls his earlier childhood fear of them, remembering he

> used to panic
> When his grey brothers scraped and fed
> Behind the hen-coop in our yard,
> On ceiling boards above my bed.

But on this occasion he stands his ground, refuses to panic, and stares the rats out. These rats are real enough to the reader as well as to the poet: "a rat / Slimed out of water,"

> He clockworked aimlessly a while,
> Stopped, back bunched and glistening,
> Ears plastered down on his knobbed skull,
> Insidiously listening.

The presence of the rats has already been prefigured at the beginning of the poem when the river itself is pictured as some slimy, cunning animal in the guise of the colours and reflections of its surroundings:

> The river nosed past,
> Pliable, oil-skinned, wearing
>
> A transfer of gables and sky.

One reviewer criticized the inappropriateness of these lines. But this is a mistaken verdict. A river may "nose" not just because it is prefiguring the creatures in the poem but because it flows into places, pushes forward and then retreats in small exploring rivulets, and the industrial pollution that floats on so many rivers is imaged in the notion of the skin of oil on the water.

We are reminded again of this polluted river towards the end of the poem when the rat crawls back into its "natural" habitat of a sewer pipe. The poet-boy sees him off, then crosses the bridge and walks away. For a short time the reader is held, like the boy, staring the experience through, and then is released to continue his progress. The sickening fear of the dark, hidden, repulsive world of the rat is overcome, in the same way that the boy comes through into a balanced recognition of his sexuality and is taken a step beyond the condition in the previous poem.

In some of the poems in the first book Heaney begins that exploration of his own relationship with the past history of his country and his family which is to become a staple theme of the later verse. One of these interesting early poems is "For the Commander of the 'Eliza'. " This is a different kind of poem from the ones so far examined. It is a dramatic monologue built around an actual historical incident—the refusal of a coastguard ship's captain to take on board six men drifting in a small boat as they searched in vain for some way to avoid starving in the potato famines in Ireland in the "hungry forties." It is a credible attempt to get inside the skin of an unpopular character who was carrying out orders which, he claimed, gave him "no mandate to relieve distress." The "Six grown men with gaping mouths and eyes" are quickly and deftly pencilled in alongside the expression of the commander's attitude. The scene is described in a predominantly curt, matter-of-fact tone suggestive of a report in the ship's log. It is clear that this style reflects not just that the commander is unable to feel some pity (although he is so limited, as the language he uses reveals in its reduction of suffering humanity to the level of bad odours—"Next day, like six bad smells, those living skulls / Drifted through . . . my ship") but also that he is the representative of the British government whose official stance is: "Less incidents the better." This view is underlined in the reprimand delivered to the commander's land-based superior who tried to order famine relief to the area. This poem is an accurate, restrained but nevertheless fierce accusation of the past wrongs done to Ireland, and it succeeds in both explaining the lack of humanity in the political sphere and making us feel the tensions between an official's carrying out of orders and the human being's sense of pity for suffering.

This poem contains the ghosts of an earlier Ireland, a tragic Ireland. In this and "Docker," a portrait of a riveter with his "Speech . . . clamped in the lips' vice," we gain glimpses of a more social, political aspect of Heaney's poetry. But in this volume he does not extend these aspects. He is more concerned with feeling his own way back through his personal past towards a community and a landscape that will help him discover his country and shape his sense of identity. Nevertheless "Docker," written before the later political violence in Northern Ireland, does contain a sad prophecy that the bitter divisions of the past could still break through:

> That fist would drop a hammer on a Catholic—
> Oh yes, that kind of thing could start again.

Two poems in particular concern the poet's relationship with his own family past: "Digging" and "Follower." Both are about the poet's father. "Digging" is also about the writing of poetry. It is the first poem in the first book and it makes clear the connection between the poet's vocation and his inherited traditions. The subject and situation are simple: sitting writing, the poet hears his old father digging beneath his window and as he watches him his memory recalls earlier childhood scenes of his father digging up potatoes and of his grandfather cutting peat. The poet recognizes that, although he has seemingly abandoned the family farm, he does "dig" on with his pen, trying to cut down into the soil of a shared existence and throw up a connection between them all. The poem is itself a discovery and a recognition of his past and an honouring of the family tradition of craftsmanship. The qualities of that tradition—its physical and sensuous pleasures in a life lived naturally and in touch with the land—are the qualities that Heaney seeks to preserve in his poems.

The link between the poet's deliberate and conscious attempt to create his own poetic identity and the nature of those family traditions is made explicit in the description of his father among the flowerbeds. He

> comes up twenty years away
> Stooping in rhythm through potato drills
> Where he was digging.

So that

> Between my finger and my thumb
> The squat pen rests.
> I'll dig with it.

The poem is to capture the rhythm of a fast-disappearing tradition and in so doing allow the poet to lay hold on his own sense of self. Thus we begin to realize that *Death of a Naturalist* not only explores the transformation of boy into man, farmer into poet, but also reckons with the gradual displacement of a traditional rural life which was close to natural sources. The whole volume is "digging" in the sense that the act of writing is an un-earthing of the poet's past and the historical roots of a nation. Heaney is uncovering a sense of selfhood and nationhood:

> The cold smell of potato mould, the squelch and slap
> Of soggy peat, the curt cuts of an edge
> Through living roots awaken in my head.
> But I've no spade to follow men like them.

That these living roots are important becomes clearer in "Follower" in which the poet pictures his father ploughing, "His shoulders globed like a full sail strung / Between the shafts and the furrow." This extravagant sim-ile begins a poem which celebrates the strength, expertise and craft of the poet's father. Heaney recalls how as a boy he "stumbled in his hob-nailed wake" (the sailing image implicitly continued) and how he then wished for nothing more than to grow up and take over his landed inheritance. Then

> I was a nuisance, tripping, falling,
> Yapping always. But today
> It is my father who keeps stumbling
> Behind me, and will not go away.

A follower as a boy, he is now dogged by memories of his father and must in turn follow the family tradition in his verse, straining with his father's energy to capture the craft and expertise of the poet in the tight traditional rhythms and rhymes of the ballad-like form of this poem. The sense of craft is the only remaining link across the generations. Pursuing the past in this way Heaney shows his sense of its durable qualities but also asserts a chang-ing tradition through his own very different vocation.

ENTRY INTO THE BURIED LIFE

Heaney's second volume, *Door into the Dark,* continues the search of the family past initiated in the first book and begins to look towards some of the thematic material of the later poems. The evocative title might seem to suggest some kind of move towards the unknown, or death, or into the subconscious, but these poems of rural landscapes, traditional crafts and village communities suggest a slightly different movement. There are two particular, but related, ways in which these poems are doors into the dark. In the first there are poems like "A Wife's Tale" and "Mother" which de-velop the technique begun in "For the Commander of the 'Eliza' " and which try to peer into the darkness of the personality of someone very different from the poet and yet someone who has grown from the same tradition as the poet. In the second way into the dark are those poems which look further into the natural processes of country life, into the dark interior of earth, nature, nature's forms, and the rituals man has created upon them (for example, "A Lough Neagh Sequence"). By living within the landscape, being part of it and by seeing through it into the lives of those dependent upon it (the farming and fishing community), the poet explores the rich, dark inheritance of his country. In the final poems of the volume the processes of nature in the peatbogs of Ireland are examined as part of the mysterious, black heart of the country's history and its people's identity.

"The Forge" is a sonnet which celebrates the craftsmanship of a village blacksmith. This is the complete poem:

> All I know is a door into the dark.
> Outside, old axles and iron hoops rusting;
> Inside, the hammered anvil's short-pitched ring,
> The unpredictable fantail of sparks
> Or hiss when a new shoe toughens in water.
> The anvil must be somewhere in the centre,
> Horned as a unicorn, at one end square,
> Set there immoveable: an altar
> Where he expends himself in shape and music.
> Sometimes, leather-aproned, hairs in the nose,
> He leans out on the jamb, recalls a clatter
> Of hoofs where traffic is flashing in rows;
> Then grunts and goes in, with a slam and flick
> To beat real iron out, to work the bellows.

The precise and unadorned diction of this poem represents as honest a piece of craftsmanship as the subject it describes. From first to last, images of sight and sound predominate: sight in lines 1–2, 4–6, 10–11; hearing in lines 3, 5, 9, 11, 13–14. Between them they encapsulate the setting and the action. But more than just the particulars of a deftly sketched description emerges with the central simile of the unicorn. This appears at first because of the visual metaphor, but the suggestion of the unicorn's horn reminds us of the unique, rare quality of the blacksmith's craft. The "shape and music" of his art is plainly stated and thereafter in the reference to "an altar" we perceive the almost religious dedication of the craftsman to his traditional skills. He is a man of few words who has little regard for the flash of cars that streak by where his horses used to go. He turns away, with unmistakable disdain for the modern world, to beat "the real iron out," and in that one small word "réal" a disparaging colour is thrown over all the inferior products of mass production—a doomed disdain for the world which will slowly, inevitably relieve him of his dedication. The door into the dark is also the way into the oblivion of a future in which such traditions will be cancelled.

There is no need to make large claims for this short poem; it does not have a large public or political sweep and in fact does not explore the dramatic qualities of the social theme it implies. But it is accurate, it does come alive as it records the last moments of a dying craft, and after it has been read it lingers in the mind to recall that even after the last blacksmith has gone "The anvil must be somewhere in the centre," if only as an image of the rich potency of such a dedication to any excellence of a craft, be it smithying or writing.

In "The Wife's Tale" Heaney takes a monologue form again and applies it to a farmer's wife as she takes out a meal to the menfolk who are bringing home the harvest. The poem begins with her description of the scene as she spreads a linen cloth under the shade of the hedge and listens to "The human gulp of the thresher [as it] ran down." But it is the poet's voice rather than his character's which talks of the sudden silence and the momentarily loud sound of "their boots / Crunching the stubble twenty yards away."

This poem is in four short parts, and in the second part we overhear the raffish banter of the husband as he makes light-hearted fun of his wife and shows off a little to his friends (and yet at the same time we perceive a genuine admiration and pride in his words):

> 'Give these fellows theirs.
> I'm in no hurry,' plucking grass in handfuls
> And tossing it in the air. . . .
>
> 'I declare a woman could lay out a field
> Though boys like us have little call for cloths.'
> He winked, then watched me as I poured a cup.

These lines quickly sketch the established roles of the sexes in the farming community—the man with his strength and disdain of comfort, the woman with her small attempts to add grace and civilizing values to a basic existence. The man's pride in the harvest and his desire to share his good fortune with his wife leads him to tell her to "Away over there and look" at the results of their labour. Then in the third part the wife runs her hands through the corn "hard as shot / Innumerable and cool." After this recognition of the "good yield" the men turn away from her, her part is done, and she moves away with the unbitter realization of her dismissal from her husband to return to her different role, leaving the men at ease "spread out, unbuttoned, grateful, under the trees."

There is in this poem a perfect grasp of relationships in a rural community, and in the careful delineation of their talk and behaviour there is a subtle placing of the value and limitations of these relationships. It is not romanticized. But it must be added that the intention of making the poem a tale told by the wife is a fiction. It is Heaney's voice and a poet's eye that selects the images and creates the tone. Only in the briefly quoted words of the man is there the genuine idiom of a character outside the poet.

"A Lough Neagh Sequence" is a long poem composed of seven short lyrics, each of which describes the fishermen or the eels that they catch, or the watery landscape of Lough Neagh. It is one of the most accomplished poems in this collection, and each separate part gains by being placed together with the other poems even though each poem is complete in itself. There is no strict development of action or great modulation in tone and mood throughout the sequence, yet the whole is not long enough for this to be felt as a limitation. Here is a cycle of thematic material which is not over-laboured and which gives a sense of completeness and roundness to the sequence. The themes are not pursued in detail but appear more as motifs or tropes which are announced in the first line and then continue to recur like the undertow of the currents in the Lough—an undramatic but persistent flow. The theme is: "The lough will claim a victim every year." The sequence is not directly about these victims but about the struggle of the fishermen to make their livelihood, the life cycle of the eels which spawn in the Lough and the children who love to catch them, one of whom was the young poet. In their various ways all are victims of the lough, not because they drown but because it absorbs them and they absorb it, carrying it in every step of their lives. It is present even in the poet's boyhood when in "Vision" (the last poem) he remembers having been threatened that

> Unless his hair was fine-combed
> The lice, they said, would gang-up
> Into a mealy rope
> And drag him, small, dirty, doomed
>
> Down to the water.

Yet eventually he is claimed by this water not in this distasteful way but by his boyhood's years spent in the marshy fields "at night when eels / Moved through the grass like hatched fears / Towards the water." The brillant transformation of the opening image of the rope of lice into the flow of eels in the lines quoted above, and then into "his world's live girdle" and "horrible cable" of the following final stanza, firmly claims the poet as "victim" of the lough, its fishing community, their traditions, and behaviour.

The different parts of the poem employ varying forms, from a basic iambic four-line stanza, through three-line stanzas rhyming *abb,* to another rhyming *aaa/bbb* and a freer two-/three-stress line. All of these (but especially the second poem on the spawning of the eels and the fourth poem on the fishermen) create a tight, vigorous pull of feelings which rise at moments to descriptions touched with a sense of vision. One such moment occurs in this description of the eel that burrows in the land during the day and suddenly reappears at night:

> Dark
> delivers him hungering
> down each undulation.

Another such moment occurs in the fifth poem, when the fishermen haul in their catch of eels as they are

> slapped into the barrel numb

> But knits itself, four-ply,
> With the furling, slippy
> Haul, a knot of back and pewter belly

> That stays continually one
> For each catch they fling in
> Is sucked home like lubrication.

The sheer physical presence of this compressed imagery is astonishing.

The sequence as a whole successfully fuses Heaney's love of his rural roots and of the people who still live in the countryside with his sense of awe at the mystery of the dark interior of the land (for which the strange, extravagant life cycle of the eel is an excellent symbol), and shows his talent for bodying forth with physical presence the subject of his descriptions. This poem looks ahead to some of the later attempts to use sequences to tie together a range of different impressions.

A further poem, "Requiem for the Croppies," takes a historical incident as its source. It is written as if spoken by the rebellious "croppies" who in an earlier period revolted against the landlords and who lived on the run until, at Vinegar Hill, they were mown down. The closeness of these people to the land is what the poet emphasizes as he describes them on the run and living off the crops—people who, when they died, would sift down to become the very land from which the crops would spring. The political theme and the restrained irony of the idea behind the poem are more evident than usual in Heaney's earlier poetry. But this image of the soil of Ireland literally containing the blood and bones of its past is to become a central symbol in his later poems.

Another later symbol which is first announced in this book is that of the peat bogs and their surrounding landscape (for example, "Bann Clay" and "Bogland"). The clay may be "baked white in the sun" but it hoards all kinds of "Mesolithic flints," scraps of the past which can suddenly be shovelled up by a boy who is simply involved in cleaning a field drain:

> This smooth weight. I labour
> Towards it still. It holds and gluts.

It is as if the key to the past of the whole race is in the grip of the land. In all senses the soil gives the community its roots and life.

Similarly the peat bogs have the property of preserving intact whatever falls into them. "The ground itself is kind" and as it keeps

> Melting and opening underfoot,
> Missing its last definition
> By millions of years

it constitutes a "wet centre" that is bottomless. This provides the last image of this book. It is as if we had come in by the door of the old rural life and had fallen out down a shaft into the bottomless dark pit of the land itself.

Door into the Dark confirms the adroit skill of handling image, rhythm and language that was revealed in the first book, but it adds a deepening theme. These poems develop a tautness of line and a spareness of language which is no less rich nor vibrant than the earlier book but which also opens up a depth and resonance that set "the dark echoing." At their best these poems rise beyond mere observations towards an emotional exploration and evaluation of a subject which has increasingly moved from the identity of the poet to the nature of Ireland herself.

THE HEART OF A LAND

More space has been devoted to the first two books than will be to

Wintering Out and *North,* not because they are considered better or more important but simply because they are easiest for a new reader to assimilate and form the indispensable groundwork for a full appreciation of the poet's aims in the later work. This work leads away from the personal and narrower confines of the poet's own past and towards the wider, public inheritance of the country's history. It is felt by Heaney to be an inheritance that is deep and sometimes violent. Certainly in poems written after 1970 there is an increasing recognition of the political troubles of Northern Ireland (although some of the most political poems have not yet been collected into book form). Yet it is not simply the acknowledgement of the facts of social division nor the terror of the Troubles that makes *North* important. It is important because in this volume, as in parts of the previous one, Heaney relates past and present, his personal past and the country's history, in order to get beneath the dangerously oversimplified political perspectives on Ireland and its people. He maintains the poet's traditional role of guardian of the "word-hoard," that deep repository of a people's reality and their dreams. Through this commitment to a continuity of past and present explored in the language of people and place, Heaney begins to discover an identity for himself that acknowledges his own part in a strife-torn land but which does not take the easy way of identifying himself with that side of history to which his birth would align him. The ground (literally in the poems about the soil of Ireland) on which he has chosen to stand is beyond, or rather beneath, the normal divisions and inevitably exposes him to the ridicule and hatred of those on any side who believe salvation lies in being partisan. It leaves him to appear as either enemy or deserter. It is not any easy stance but he draws his courage from the fact that ultimately it is the only stance that can include the whole of Ireland—the only possibility for resolution.

The strain of this lonely task is seen in *Wintering Out,* where many poems, although not overtly political in subject, are about the estrangement and isolation that the poet feels ("Servant Boy," "The Last Mummer," "The Wool Trade," "Shore Woman" and "Bye-Child"). In them the poet identifies with various conditions of alienation in others, and they seem to reflect a suggestion that he is circling round some deep centre in himself which he has not yet clearly traced, touched or understood. In other poems that are concerned with places and the language of the names of places (the words that begin to put him in touch with the "word-hoard") there is also this feeling of a search for some stable centre. A glance at "Servant Boy" and "The Last Mummer," together with a closer look at "Gifts of Rain," may make this link between people and place clearer.

"Servant Boy," consisting of five unrhymed four-line stanzas, is an uncomplicated poem which communicates a sense of the bitter independence concealed by the docile competence of the servant's outward behaviour. He works on a farm or great house which has its own outhouses and chicken runs. In the poem he is seen collecting eggs and wandering through the stables and into "the back doors of the little / barons" to bring "the warm eggs." He is an "Old work-whore, slave- / blood" who must be at the beck and call of his masters and yet who has still learnt to hug to himself a free, private self that he keeps safely from the knowledge of his masters: he "kept your patience / and your counsel." He is pictured "wintering out" at "the back-end of a bad year," and the poem swings round the contrast between his cold, outcast situation and his role as the delicate bearer of "warm eggs." Parallel to this dark/light and cold/warm contrast is the poet's relationship with the boy with whom he clearly identifies:

> how
> you draw me into
> your trail. Your trail
>
> broken from haggard to stable,
> a straggle of fodder
> stiffened on snow,
> comes first-footing
>
> the back doors of the little
> barons:

The association of "first-footing" with New Year rituals suggests the boy is more than just a servant in the poet's eyes. He is an isolated figure, outside his society; yet he has kept his heart and mind clear, untrammelled by the condition of slavery to which that society has reduced him. In fact that society, unknown to its masters, is utterly dependent on the slave's ability to keep the eggs warm—to bring its source of life and sustenance. As such he becomes an image of the poet who feels unable to identify with any one part of his society and who is trying to discover and restore the sources of life beneath his country's divided powers.

Historically a mummer is an actor who roamed the country or appeared at Christmas and the New Year to act out the rituals of the season in a traditional "automatic style" and with a "curiously hypnotizing impressiveness," according to Thomas Hardy. In Heaney's "The Last Mummer" we have a poem of light, clear two-lined verses with a minimum of

punctuation and the lightest of regular stress beats, which allows the mummer to move rapidly through the poem. He appears almost as a ghostly
memory, an insubstantial creature and creator of dreams and visions who
wanders the countryside and "Moves out of the fog / on the lawn, pads up
the terrace" to the great house, "beating / the bars of the gate" to demand
entrance to perform the regular rituals that will remind the inhabitants of
his magical powers. He takes on a mysterious, unanchored form in this
poem, being close to nature and the repository of the language of all
communities:

> His tongue went whoring
>
> among the civil tongues,
> he had an eye for weather-eyes
>
> at cross-roads and lane-ends
> and could don manners
>
> at a flutter of curtains.

Protean, he takes the shape of any part. He is magic—"His straw mask
and hunch were fabulous"—and he could escape the politicians and their
attendant strident divisions of opinion by the cunning of his craft as enter-
tainer and magician who can manipulate reality for the conviction of all
sides. He is master of all realities:

> He came trammelled
> in the taboos of the country
>
> picking a nice way through
> the long toils of blood
>
> and feuding.

He leaves the poet dreaming of "a line of mummers," precursors of the poet
who "untousled a first dewy path / Into the summer grazing." Again the
poet is identifying with someone apart from his society who nevertheless
performs an indispensable service for that society through their deep alle-
giance to the secrets of the country's traditions. It is this that gives him
the power to thread a path through the blood and feuding.

Through these poems Heaney expresses his being forced as an artist
away from his community and yet, because the roots of his art lie in the
life of that community and its traditions, he believes he must continue a
search for some way to remain fiercely independent so that he can play the

true servant to his community as the magus who can create the community's dream and make "dark tracks" between its members and the deep springs of their lives.

Some of the other poems in this collection concern themselves with the names of places: "Anahorish," "Toome," "Broagh." The language of the place-names is identified with the tongue of the land and the speech of the poet:

> *Anahorish,* soft gradient
> of consonant, vowel-meadow,
>
> after-image of lamps
> swung through the yards
> on winter evenings.

We begin to see in this poem the use of names, of language as metaphor and symbol for Ireland and its past. We begin to register Heaney's fusing of place, people, politics, past, and poetry. On its own this poem does not go so far. Here the "place of clear water" is no more than an after-image of the past community which burns gently, if not brightly, in the syllables of the present name. But in "Gifts of Rain" we have the explicit handling of this extended metaphor of language history. It is not a poem of statement, but a vigorous description of the land lashed by storm, written in a loose-limbed stanza pattern which, being more open than Heaney's previous style, seems able to catch the downpour of a cloudburst and rush it on through the runnels of the poem as it rises to a swift flood that gives a sense of the movement of the water. In it there is no clutter of adjectives and adverbs to describe the man working through the downpour and experiencing himself as part of the elements:

> So
>
> he is hooped to where he planted
> and sky and ground
>
> are running naturally among his arms
> that grope the cropping land.

The rain "world-schooled" the poet's ear, and turning to the farmers, he becomes aware of his distance from those who crop the land and of his need to reawaken some sense of continuity between himself and the past, the people and the land.

> I cock my ear
> at an absence—
> in the shared calling of the blood
>
> arrives my need
> for antediluvian lore.
> Soft voices of the dead
> are whispering by the shore

As he listens to the water of "the Moyola harping on / its gravel beds" he is visited by a vision of "The tawny guttural water" as it seems to him to spell itself, and he sees it "bedding the locale / in the utterance." The swollen river breathes "through vowels and history." In this looser, freer style of line with its pared-down language, Heaney is beginning to transpose description by exposition into a truly metaphorical, symbolic level of meaning where the meaning cannot exist apart from its image in the poem, in just the same way as he comes to believe that the meaning of the voices of the dead cannot be separated from the living waters of the Moyola. He is developing a technique that will defeat clumsy commentary. The poems will not mean, but be. So it is in another poem about a place that he says

> My mouth holds round
> the soft blastings,
> *Toome, Toome,*
> as under the dislodged
>
> slab of the tongue
> I push into a souterrain

and thus he speaks the land becomes "sleeved in / alluvial mud." In "Broagh," too, he speaks a language that is composed of the place, and the poetry and place interfuse to capture the land's identity and make it his own.

In *Wintering Out* he writes out of this land, the people and places that he has always spoken of, but the need to know them becomes more and more acute as he increasingly writes out the memories of his own childhood. "A Northern Hoard" and "Traditions" make it clear that there is a search now for a way back from the personal poems of his own past towards the past of a whole country. The urgency of this search is revealed in the dedicatory poem written after he had seen a new prison camp for the internees. Seeing this he feels that "we hug our little destiny again." Ireland's new troubles remain the same as the old ones and Heaney suggests the poet's task also remains the same. The poet must use his craft to bring an order to the chaos of divided feelings, to grasp and hold both sides of the struggle, to speak for the past, dead Ireland and in so doing to create a new song out of the deeper destiny of the country that links past and present to reveal its "coherent miseries."

It is *North* that really begins to provide the sense of that centre to his identity around which Heaney seems to have been circling. In it he pursues the honing of his style begun in the previous volume and in the clean, clear sweep of these poems the continuities and coherences really begin to be gathered up.

The title poem presents the poet looking out over the Atlantic from "a long strand, / the hammered shod of a bay" from where he hears "the secular / powers" of the sea and can look north towards Iceland. Standing there he is well placed geographically and metaphorically to look into the cold heart of northern Europe. His mind fills with the "violence and epiphany" of the Norsemen who linked Iceland, Greenland, Scandinavia, and Ireland, and he remembers the tombs, monuments, and relics of that warrior race scattered between Orkney and Dublin in museums and in

> the solid
> belly of stone ships,
> those hacked and glinting
> in the gravel of thawed streams.

These memories crowd together and link war, travel, and trade, "thick-witted couplings and revenges," whose memory incubates spilled blood. The past is redolent with the same violent revenges as the present. But to the poet these northern histories and legends, landscapes and hatreds, travels and tongues, are all contained in that "long strand" which is the essence of Ireland. The Atlantic that bore the longboats with their "swimming tongue . . . buoyant with hindsight" is to the poet a source of "secular powers" which can replace the religious bigotry that is at root of the long history of violence because that ocean *precedes* all religious differences. The land was there before man. The poem ends with the "longship's swimming tongue" pronouncing invocation and command:

> 'Lie down

> in the word-hoard, burrow
> the coil and gleam
> of your furrowed brain.

> Compose in darkness.
> Expect aurora borealis

in the long foray
but no cascade of light.

Keep your eye clear
at the bleb of the icicle,
trust the feel of what nubbed treasure
your hands have known.'

The poet is to dig down into the past, beneath even the violent history, to close with the earth and sea that clutches and drowns remnants of the past (wrecks, flints in pebbles, bodies preserved in the peat bogs—each of which have poems to themselves elsewhere in the latest volumes). He must cling to what he already knows, to what the land preserves; he is to search out the "word-hoard" of this ancient language.

The form of this poem is sparse and ribbed compared with the heavier, more opulent language of the earliest poems. The lean line and free rhythm (a basic two-/three-stress system) are given more power by the diction. From the metaphor of the rocky shore ("hammered shod of a bay") to the cool, bright light of the aurora borealis, we are presented with a pattern of imagery that suggests cold, hard edges and which captures the landscape and its climate, the nature of the Norse raiders and the poet's determination.

The "word-hoard" is explicitly stated in this poem, and it begins to call up threads from other poems, such as "Anahorish," which have also used the language metaphor to connect place and past with the poet's task. This metaphor becomes dominant as a symbol over this whole volume. The poet speaks, but the land, its history, objects and people speak through him in each poem.

A further symbol of continuity is developed in "Tollund Man" in the previous book and in *North* is firmly established as a controlling metaphor in several of the best poems. These are about the peat bogs' peculiar power to preserve whatever falls into them. They are full of relics of Ireland's past, including bodies (usually of those who have been murdered or have otherwise met a violent end). This natural phenomenon links the landscape with the people and with the rural past of Heaney's own family who, like many rural families, cut peat for themselves and to make a living. Of this image Heaney has written: "So I began to get an idea of the bog as the memory of the landscape, or as a landscape that remembered everything that happened in it and to it."

It is impossible to describe the sharp, physical sense of the bogs and their buried "treasure" except by quotation:

My body was braille
for the creeping influences:
dawn suns groped over my head . . .

the seeps of winter
digested me, . . .

I knew winter cold
like the nuzzle of fjords
at my thighs—

               ("Bog Queen")

    The grain of his wrists
    is like bog oak,
    the ball of his heel

    like a basalt egg.
    ("The Grauballe Man")

These bodies of people killed by violence who yet remain, preserved perma-
nently in the horrible attitudes of death—

    I can feel the tug
    of the halter at the nape
    of her neck, the wind
    on her naked front
           ("Punishment")

—are perfect images for Ireland's troubles past and present, and for the persistence of the violent past in the present. In "Punishment" Heaney pro-
poses this most explicitly as he writes of his sympathy for the young girl
who was hanged as an adulteress and who was one of the bodies discovered
in the bogs. He acknowledges that, although "I almost love you," if he
had lived at the time of her trouble he would have remained silent at her
fate, even if he knew it was wrong, and would not have been prepared to
take sides to defend her. In the same way he cannot speak out directly to
plead for those girls branded as traitors in modern Ireland because they
have fallen in love with British soldiers. He has been unable to speak when
they have been punished by being tarred-and-feathered by sectarian groups:

    I who have stood dumb
    when your betraying sisters,
    cauled in tar,
    wept by the railings,

> who would connive
> in civilized outrage
> yet understand the exact
> and tribal, intimate revenge.

Here we begin to understand what Heaney is trying to do in these images of continuity. His isolation—his sense of being outside and yet connected still to Ireland's troubles (victim and yet also related to the perpetrators of the violence)—is seen in this poem, and in this whole volume, as a necessary stand for the artist. The poet's imagination (his mummer's power to enter into the lives of the many) takes him through his family past to the dark peat core of Ireland where he experiences life as both invader and invaded, revenger and victim. It prevents him from taking sides, "and in the process someone is betrayed" by this "artful voyeur" who must accept his own punishment by standing fast to the "word-hoard," even though he suffers the derision of those who condemn him for not making a plainer political response. The artist's role, Heaney insists, is to stand on all sides and to accept "the mire and complexities" of the blood of a whole people.

All the poems that dig after ancient Ireland, the island of the north, of Viking inheritance, especially those about the bogs, are gathered up in "Kinship." In this taught and controlled poem the language is simple but penetrating, a statement predominantly of noun and verb:

> I love this turf-face
> its black incisions,
> the cooped secrets
> of process and ritual;

On this land of his kin he declares "I step through origins." It is ground that is "outback of my mind" and provides him with a "centre [that] holds / and spreads." The "melting grave" of the bog is "vowel of earth," contains "mutations of weathers / and seasons" and though "sour with the blood" of Ireland's past it is "the goddess [who] swallows / our love and terror." It is the land he feels closest to, it is the land that literally preserves all that falls into it, and the poet chooses to stand there and, paradoxically, stands firm by allowing himself to be sucked down into its dark interior.

Whether this is a real resolution or whether it is only a fiction depends upon the individual's response. For some readers a fiction—the imaginative reconstruction of a world connected with reality but not synonymous with it—may be the only kind of resolution possible in a deeply troubled world and the only way left for preparing the ground for the growth of a new and solving insight.

North is an ambitious book. It is written in a quiet but persistently penetrating tone, a hard but not colourless style. It is far from the luxuriant growth of the first book in terms of technique but it was nevertheless prepared for in those previous volumes. The early poems of childhood and growing up provided Heaney with the first strong foundations on which to feel what it was to be a poet in Ireland. From these he learnt to trace his origins further and further back into his country's past. That is why the two tender dedicatory poems of *North* remain directed at his family and his family's native countryside. Heaney has talked of his poetry as the revelation of identity:

> poetry as revelation of the self to the self, as the restoration
> of the culture to itself; poems as elements of continuity, with the
> aura and authenticity of archaeological finds, where the buried
> shard has an importance that is not obliterated by the buried city.

He has set himself a daunting task in attempting to do this. In the dedicatory poems he writes of "our anonymities" (the common experiences which are shared by all but which are rarely spoken of) and the preservation of these which is the essence of any true culture. In the last poem of *North* he hints, through characteristically rural imagery, at the object of his task and its gains and losses (a "wood-kerne" is a foot soldier (usually a peasant) who has taken to the woods to escape capture).

> I am neither internee nor informer;
> An inner émigré, grown long-haired
> And thoughtful; a wood-kerne
>
> Escaped from the massacre,
> Taking protective colouring
> From bole and bark, feeling
> Every wind that blows;

JAY PARINI

The Ground Possessed

In "Ocean's Love to Ireland," from Seamus Heaney's recent volume *North,* Ireland is itself likened to a ruined maid undone by Ocean, who has "scattered her dream of fleets." The Spanish prince "has spilled his gold / And failed her." Now "iambic drums / Of English beat the woods," and her poets sink like Onan, From all sides, the island is under seige, her dainty farthingale lifted by Ocean's lecherous fingers "like a scarf of weed lifting / In the front of a wave." As always, she heels under pressure, tugs her forelock and speaks with pure English vowels. But she remains inviolable from within, her "ground possessed and repossessed."

North is a major accomplishment, a book-length sequence of lyrics which exploits the metaphor of possession more fully than any other Irish poet has done. The poems are richly autobiographical, yet the poet consistently weaves the particulars of his life into a mythic frame; he has evolved a unique species of political poetry which refers at once to the current Irish "troubles" and to the human situation generally. One would have to invoke Pablo Neruda's *Heights of Macchu Picchu* for a parallel. Consequently, I think Heaney is among the finest poets writing today in English, and I shall examine his work to date to support my large claim for him. His poetry has evolved with remarkable integrity from the beginning. He has drawn ever widening concentric rings around the first few themes he circled; his language has grown steadily more dense, more resonant, more singularly his own with each successive volume. And now, at the height of his powers, one awaits each new book with the same expectancy afforded Yeats and Eliot in their middle years.

From *The Southern Review* 16, no. 1 (January 1980). © 1980 by Jay Parini. Originally entitled "Seamus Heaney: The Ground Possessed."

Heaney comes from the north, from Derry, and his first book conjured the pastoral topography of his childhood on the farm. One should remember, of course, that even Theocritus and Virgil did not write for country folk, to put it mildly; rather, they evinced the atmosphere of rural life for the benefit of cultivated city dwellers who would appreciate the subtle texture of meaning embedded in their eclogues. This is the pastoral tradition, and Heaney's *Death of a Naturalist* (1966) fits into it. He *was* in fact a farm boy, and he writes from immediate experience; but his craft was learned in the city, at Queens University, Belfast, where he enjoyed the tutelage of Philip Hobsbaum, the poet-critic, among others. Hobsbaum's bias toward lean, physical language wedded to intellectual toughness shows up in Heaney's early work, as in the first lines of "Digging":

> Between my finger and my thumb
> The squat pen rests: snug as a gun.
>
> Under my window, a clear rasping sound
> When the spade sinks into gravelly ground:
> My father, digging. I look down
>
> Till his straining rump among the flowerbeds
> Bends low, comes up twenty years away
> Stooping in rhythm through potato drills
> Where he was digging.

Heaney furls us into his vision with lines admitting no abstraction; his experience thrusts itself upon us directly, and we cannot doubt "the cold smell of potato mould, the squelch and slap / Of soggy peat, the curt cuts of an edge." The violence of Heaney's sight, which holds each image firmly in the mind as a butterfly in pincers, looks forward to the line from "Fosterage" in *North:* "Description is revelation." Like Wordsworth, who says in *The Prelude* that he was "fostered alike by beauty and by fear," this poet lays claim to a similar parentage.

The title poem, "Death of a Naturalist," recollects a frightening instance when the poet as a boy was confronted by a horde of frogs attending their spawn, which he used to steal every spring in his role of amateur naturalist:

> I would fill jampotfuls of the jellied
> Specks to range on window-sills at home,
> On shelves at school, and wait and watch until
> The fattening dots burst into nimble-
> Swimming tadpoles.

This (of course) angered the frogs, so they invaded the flax-dam to avenge the youthful offender:

> The air was thick with a brass chorus.
> Right down the dam gross-bellied frogs were cocked
> On sods; their loose necks pulsed like sails. Some hopped:
> The slap and plop were obscene threats. Some sat
> Poised like mud grenades, their blunt heads farting.

Heaney's shocking phrases, like "their blunt heads farting," avoid being gratuitous because of the charged atmosphere present from the outset: "All year the flax-dam festered in the heart / Of the townland." "Festered" prepares us for a strong succession of verbs: "sweltered," "gargled," "croaked," "pulsed," and so on. The reader's eye tends obsessively to the verbs, which claw and pick at the attention and funnel us through each poem. The accuracy of every natural detail lends an authority to Heaney's voice; when he explains, "You could tell the weather by frogs too / For they were yellow in the sun and brown / In rain," we believe him implicitly.

Death of a Naturalist is an apprentice volume, one in which a young poet tests the limits of his abilities, tries out various verse forms and metrical patterns. But if there are echoes in these poems, they are well assimilated. A major poet often steps into his own clearing from the start, and Heaney does this here. The controlled irony of "The Early Purges," with its adumbration of things to come in later volumes, shows this young writer possessed of a maturity beyond his years. The poem recounts another childhood instance, a time when Dan Taggart drowned some kittens, " 'the scaggy wee shits,' " in a bucket of stinging cold water:

> "Sure isn't it better for them now?"
> Like wet gloves they bobbed and shone till he sluiced
> Them out on the dunghill, glossy and dead.
> Suddenly frightened, for days I sadly hung
> Round the yard, watching the three sogged remains
> Turn mealy and crisp as old summer dung
> Until I forgot them.

Yet the fear returns when Dan pursues a mean vendetta against living creatures: rats and rabbits, crows and hens. The poet, half believing himself, asserts that "living displaces false sentiments"; nonetheless a heavy irony in the last line fumes like invisible, sharply scented smoke: "But on well-run farms pests have to be kept down." None of the sentimental flurries characteristic of Yeats as a novice can be found in Heaney; he writes with a stern grip on reality that makes *The Tower* poems splendid.

The boyhood evoked in these poems is tinged with violence, as we have seen, but not blotted out by it. "Follower," for example, investigates a complicated father-son relationship. The opening image takes our breath away:

> My father worked with a horse-plough,
> His shoulders globed like a full sail strung
> Between shafts and the furrow.
> The horses strained at his clicking tongue.

Heaney follows through with the sailing analogy:

> His eye
> Narrowed and angled at the ground
> Mapping the furrow exactly.

Then he brings himself into the picture:

> I stumbled in his hob-nailed wake,
> Fell sometimes on the polished sod;
> Sometimes he rode me on his back
> Dipping and rising to his plod.

The poem ends with a swift reversal, for the follower is not merely the son tripping and falling behind the father.

> But today
> It is my father who keeps stumbling
> Behind me, and will not go away.

The poet, having forsaken an ancient call to the soil, cannot exorcise the father, nor will he ever.

Family deaths, the persistence of old ghosts, hunting expeditions, potato diggings, and the normal preoccupations of a life in County Derry provide material for *Death of a Naturalist;* yet the loveliest poems in the book are those addressed to Marie Heaney, the poet's wife. "Valediction" sets the standard:

> Lady with the frilled blouse
> And simple tartan skirt,
> Since you have left the house
> Its emptiness has hurt
> All thought. In your presence

Time rode easy, anchored
On a smile; but absence
Rocked love's balance, unmoored
The days. They buck and bound
Across the calendar
Pitched from the quiet sound
Of your flower-tender
Voice. Need breaks on my strand;
You've gone, I am at sea.
Until you resume command
Self is in mutiny.

The naval conceit is drawn up tight as a bootlace with the final, consummate phrase. The alternate rhymes lend polish to the otherwise roughly finished trimeter in which the rhythm mimics the theme: the unsettling effect of the beloved's absence. Not an ounce of fat detracts from the poems swift statement and hard, clear edges. It is a minor classic.

A full rhetorical flourish adorns "Poem: For Marie":

Love, I shall perfect for you the child
Who diligently potters in my brain
Digging with heavy spade till sods were piled
Or puddling through muck in a deep drain.

The poem is about fathering; the lovers come together "within one golden ring" to perfect their dreams, to flesh out their imaginings with the particulars of experience, arranging the world "within new limits." The metaphor shifts slightly in "Scaffolding," an elaborately metaphysical conceit which compares the scaffoldings erected against a wall to hold up masons at work to the emotional ramparts sustained by lovers. When the masons finish, the scaffolding naturally disappears; the poet says:

So if, my dear, there sometimes be
Old bridges breaking between you and me

Never fear. We may let the scaffolds fall
Confident that we have built our wall.

"Personal Helicon" concludes the book, and it is as good as anything Heaney has written since. It pulls into a single locus the varied themes of *Death of a Naturalist,* and it may be thought of as poetic *credo,* a guide to this poet's personal iconography. Heaney's version of Helicon, the stream

which ran from Parnassus and the source of inspiration to ancient poets, is
the well on his farm:

> As a child, they could not keep me from wells
> And old pumps with buckets and windlasses.
> I loved the dark drop, the trapped sky, the smells
> Of waterweed, fungus and dank moss.

The well of memory, with its slippery sides and musky odors, goes down
"so deep you saw no reflection in it." Like a poem, it "gave back your own
call / With a clean new music in it." This world of dangling roots and
slime, of soft mulch and scary ferns, recalls the greenhouse poems of Theodore Roethke, with whom Heaney has much in common at this stage in
his development. Here is concrete poetry with a vengeance, what Roethke
called "that anguish of concreteness." Heaney mocks his own adult preten-
sions, the priggish refusals (which he never makes) to delve into his subter-
ranean source:

> Now, to pry into roots, to finger slime,
> To stare big-eyed Narcissus, into some spring
> Is beneath all adult dignity. I rhyme
> To see myself, to set the darkness singing.

With *Door into the Dark* (1969), Heaney opens a new vein of subject
matter and works his way slowly, at times painfully, toward the mature
style fully realized in *North*. There is the expected carryover from *Death of
a Naturalist;* anything that good deserves carrying-over! The folksy, pastoral side begins to dwindle, although poems like "The Outlaw" (about an
old man named Kelly who keeps an illegal stud bull), "The Thatcher," and
"The Wife's Tale" are a fine addition to earlier poems like "Churning Day"
and "The Diviner." Heaney's geniality, compassion, and impish wit run
through these poems like a watermark. There is great precedence in British
poetry for this kind of poem, of course, and this poet adds a few fresh lyrics
to this tradition (which reaches back well beyond Wordsworth, who comes
to mind as a master of this genre). Heaney is matched among his British/
Irish contemporaries writing this kind of romantic-pastoral verse only by
R. S. Thomas and George Mackay Brown. What interests me especially
about *Door into the Dark* is Heaney's discovery of natural symbols in rural
life—which gives his work a new resonance; also, I am intrigued by the
sudden compression of style, the touch intellectual sinew flexed in phrase
after phrase, and the laser-beam focus of his vision: the image is seared in-
delibly on the reader's mind.

Heaney pushes his style toward a spareness, an absence of rhetoric and normal syntactical connective tissue, which culminates in the granite style of *Wintering Out.* "Dream," for instance, establishes the new style early in the book:

> With a billhook
> Whose head was hand-forged and heavy
> I was hacking a stalk
> Thick as a telegraph pole.
> My sleeves were rolled
> And the air fanned cool past my arms
> As I swung and buried the blade,
> Then laboured to work it unstuck.
>
> The next stroke
> Found a man's head under the hook.
> Before I woke
> I heard the steel stop
> In the bone of the brow.

The style recalls Hopkins, one of Heaney's dominant ancestors, with its heavy alliteration, "sprung" rhythm, and the tightly packed imagery. A tendency toward symbolism is also in evidence: we are given nothing but one side of most analogues, tenor without vehicle, the same technique used by Blake in early lyrics such as "The Sick Rose." Heaney supplies us with the barest image in "Dream," but the context is sufficient; the poem gathers to itself the luminosity of a natural symbol caught in the poet's energetic eye.

"The Forge," a similar poem to "Dream" and one of the best in the collection, illustrates my point about symbolism further. As a metaphor, "the crucible of art" has a long past. One thinks of Hephaestus, who crafted the shield of Achilles, or, more recently, of Joyce's Stephen Dedalus and his wish "to forge in the smithy of [his] soul the uncreated conscience of [his] race." The poem begins with a line from which the books takes its title: "All I know is a door into the dark." The suggestiveness of this line, which takes us from the literal to a metaphoric level instantly, indicates that Heaney has more in mind than simple description of a forge. This becomes clearer when he describes the anvil in religious (almost sacrificial) terms:

> Horned as a unicorn, at one end square,
> Set there immoveable: an altar
> Where he expends himself in shape and music.

The blacksmith, a modern anachronism, reminds us of the poet in today's
world:

>He leans out on the jamb, recalls a clatter
>Of hoofs where traffic is flashing in rows;
>Then grunts and goes in, with a slam and flick
>To beat real iron out, to work the bellows.

So the poet withdraws into the dark room of his imagining, beats out the
"real iron" of language into significant form. Heaney is himself a "maker"
in the old sense (from the Greek *poiein,* to make). Like Yeats, he wants
only to "hammer his thoughts into unity."

"Description is revelation"—a phrase from *North*—illumines the technique behind many of the poems in *Door into the Dark,* where each act of
description becomes a repossession of experience. Often Heaney's tone, as
in "Girls Bathing, Galway 1965," is whimsical, using bathos as a common
trope; but one finds a seriousness underlying even this light poem. It
begins:

>The swell foams where they float and crawl,
>A catherine wheel of arm and hand;
>Each head bobs curtly as a football.
>The yelps are faint here on the strand.

Yet "the breakers pour / Themselves into themselves, the years / Shuttle
through space invisibly." Generations labor "in fear of flesh and sin / For
the time has been accomplished." These pronouncements would weigh too
heavily on us were the bathers not "bare-legged, smooth-shouldered and
long-backed." Their immediate attractiveness and their ignorance of the
fact that "the time has been accomplished" work against all pretentious ef-
forts to interpret their meaning *sub specie aeternitatis.* "So Venus comes, matter-of-fact," we are told, not like Botticelli's classic maiden with her arms
full of flowers, wafting in on a shell. Revelation is matter-of-fact, almost
accidental. The poet's job is simply *to see exactly* what is in front of him.
And he must keep one foot firmly planted on the ground, like Antaeus,
who is the subject of two poems in *North.*

The remaining poems of *Door into the Dark* are closely autobiographical and anecdotal. "The Wife's Tale" and "Mother" recall the looser, colloquial style of *Death of a Naturalist,* although much of the earlier sentiment
is stripped away. "Elegy for a Stillborn Child" stands out among these
more personal poems for its startling analogies; it begins with the poet
speaking to the dead child:

> Your mother walks light as empty creel
> Unlearning the intimate nudge and pull
>
> Your trussed up weight of seed-flesh and bone-curd
> Had insisted on.

The creel simile arrests us with the image of a woman moving along, her ribs like the creel's wooden bars, all air and light; the kennings "seed-flesh" and "bone-curd" have a skaldic ring, a new aspect of Heaney's work which looks forward to *North*. "Elegy" charts the progress from husband to father, and then the disappointment of bewildered parents. The final section is a meditation on emptiness in which the poet refrains from all assertions of either despair or false hope:

> On lonely journeys I think of it all,
> Birth of death, exhumation for burial.
>
> A wreath of small clothes, a memorial pram,
> And parents reaching for a phantom limb.
>
> I drive by remote control in this bare road
> Under a drizzling sky, a circling rook,
>
> Past mountain fields, full to the brim with cloud,
> White waves riding home on a wintry lough.

One has the sense of powerful emotion held tightly in check by the formal control of Heaney's sprung pentameter and slant-rhymed couplets.

The most important poem in the book, I believe, comes last. "Bog-land" concludes *Door into the Dark* and lends additional meaning to the title, for the Irish bogs (which preserve generations of Irish civilization intact) may be thought of as openings into the dark of history. The theme of this poem is the literal repossession of the ground, a theme which becomes central in Heaney's next two books. The poet observes that because Ireland has no prairies "to slice a big sun at evening"—the horizon encroaches from all directions. "Our unfenced country," says Heaney, "is bog that keeps crusting / Between the sights of the sun." An amateur archaeologist, he tells of recent exhumations from bogs:

> They've taken the skeleton
> Of the Great Irish Elk
> Out of the peat, set it up
> An astounding crate full of air.

Butter sunk under
More than a hundred years
Was recovered salty and white.
The ground itself is kind, black butter

Melting and opening underfoot.

The suggestive possibilities of bogland seem unbounded, and Heaney
knows this; but he refuses to go much beyond a literal representation until
the last line: "The wet centre is bottomless." As a symbol of the unconscious past which must be unfolded, layer by layer, the bog image will
prove indispensable. For this reason, "Bogland" is a watershed poem in the
Heaney corpus. After it, one rereads all the poems coming before it with
a new lens, realizing that this poet's vision of historical sequence reaches
beyond the pastoral-folk tradition. The theme of digging, registered twice
in *Death of a Naturalist* (potato digging, then), moves into a rich light
now, acquiring new potency from the symbolic force of the bogland
metaphor.

In *Wintering Out* (1972) Heaney was quick to pick up the end note of
Door into the Dark, to mine the ore still locked inside this vein. Ireland's
archaeological sites yield poems like "Bog Oak," "Anahorish," and
"Toome," and Heaney's research into Danish excavations results in "The
Tollund Man" and "Nerthus." These poems exploit the metaphoric plunge
backward through time tenaciously. As one delves in bogland, history peels
away like the layers of an onion; one falls through shelves of civilizations
often represented by odds and ends such as the oak beam that was once "a
carter's trophy" in "Bog Oak." "Anahorish," which means "place of clear
water," is an ancient site where the mound-dwellers lived, a place "where
springs washed into / the shiny grass / and darkened cobbles in the lane."
Heaney evokes the pristine quality—a translucent crispness—of neolithic
life:

With pails and barrows

those mound-dwellers
go waist-deep in mist
to break the light ice
at wells and dunghills.

The poems in part 1 of this collection all reconstruct historical instances or offer a meditation on some fact of the lost past. "Servant Boy,"
for example, draws a simple portrait of a lower-class child who

comes first-footing
the back doors of the little
barons: resentful
and impenitent.

The poet clearly identifies with this "jobber among shadows." Placed where
it is, in the sequence of bog poems, "Servant Boy" stands out as a reminder
of Heaney's breadth of vision, his empathetic range. The poem recollects
the old feud between invading noblemen and the indigenous servant
classes; it helps to explain the present Irish conflict by pointing to centuries
of accrued resentment. There is nothing overtly political about "Servant
Boy," of course. Heaney stays rather far away from engagement of this sort
until *North;* but one senses the gathering storm.

The theme of "the ground possessed and repossessed" finds only
oblique expression in these poems, insofar as the theme is political. But in
"Land" the repossession is personal and literal as the poet confronts the
ground like a lover:

If I lie with my ear
in this loop of silence

long enough, thigh-bone
and shoulder against the ground,

I expect to pick up
a small drumming

and must not be surprised
in bursting air

to find myself snared, swinging
an ear ring of sharp wire.

One "picks up a drumming" from the land, he says: the poet's alliterative
drumming, perhaps, or the pulse of history muffled in the loam. The poet,
with his ear-ring, is marked by his curious affectation, his art, which
pierces his ear uncomfortably and snares him. In "Gifts of Rain," which
follows "Land," he says:

I cock my ear
at an absence—
in the shared calling of blood

arrives my need
for antediluvian lore.

> Soft voices of the dead
> are whispering by the shore.

The desire for "antediluvian lore" drives Heaney, in "Toome," back
into the trench:

> I push into a souterrain
> prospecting what new
> in a hundred centuries'
>
> loam, flints, musket-balls,
> fragmented ware,
> torcs and fish-bones
> till I'm sleeved in
> alluvial mud that shelves
> suddenly under
> bog water and tributaries,
> and elvers tail my hair.

One finds not the slightest excess in any of these poems; Heaney's rhetoric
errs, if at all, on the side of spareness. His diction, sprung from a serious
philological delving, reminds one of Emerson's speculations in "The Poet":

> The poets made all the words, and therefore language is the ar-
> chives of history . . . a sort of tomb of the muses. For though
> the origin of most of our words is forgotten, each word was at
> first a stroke of genius, and obtained currency because for the
> moment it symbolized the world to the first speaker and to the
> hearer. The etymologist finds the deadest word to have been
> once a brilliant picture. Language is fossil poetry.

The poet's job, then, is to restore language to its meaning, its pictorial
essence. Thus, Heaney examines each word carefully: *Toome, Broagh,* or *Anahorish,* that "place of clear water." He is the poet-as-archaeologist, reviv-
ing a lost past, and using the past to inform a cloudy present as "we hug
our little destiny again."

In "Traditions," he complains: "Our guttural muse / was bulled long
ago / by the alliterative tradition" and makes fun of such English words as
"varsity" and "deem." England, John Bull, has long since replaced the Celtic tradition with the one Heaney now writes in; Irish poetry is now a sub-
division of English poetry. This displacement of traditions is one aspect of
the "the ground possessed," and Heaney's "repossession" involves remaking
the language, grafting into it words which have been bulled under. This

also involves a willful distortion of the mellifluous English iamb. The poems in *Wintering Out* are made of gristle and bone, of rock and water; they are redolent of Irish soil and what Hopkins called "the taste of self." Hopkins' own efforts to revive the rhythms of Anglo-Saxon verse resemble Heaney's experiments with "the guttural muse."

Part 2 of *Wintering Out* moves away from the wide historical rummage of part 1 into the private arena of one man's life; I prefer the poems in this section on the whole, no doubt because they are less dense, less tortuously argued. "Wedding Day" sets the new tone:

> I am afraid.
> Sound has stopped in the day
> And the images reel over
> And over. Why all those tears,
>
> The wild grief on his face
> Outside the taxi? The sap
> Of mourning rises
> In our waving guests.

The terrified groom sees his new wife behind the tall cake "like a deserted bride" who would still go on with the ritual in spite of her husband's departure. He runs into the "gents" to find on the walls "a skewered heart / And a legend of love." This ancient image brings him to his senses, and he says to his bride: "Let me sleep on your breast to the airport," subsuming like a child to a power greater than himself; whether it be the feminine principle or simply the inevitability of experience, we cannot say. What matters is the gentle submission tendered by the groom's request.

"Summer Home" is a major sequence and the emotional center of part 2; in it Heaney explores the vicissitudes of love and its attendant permutations and distortions. The poet begins by recollecting a scene in a foreign country, a time when everything was out of joint:

> Was it wind off the dump
> or something in heat
> dogging us, the summer gone soon, a foul nest incubating
>   somewhere?

Something larval, alive, is discovered under the doormat and has to be scalded dead. This emblematic gesture profers the possibility of cure, of reconciliation between man and climate, between man and woman. The second section images the husband "bushing the door" with an armload of wild cherries and rhododendron. His wife sobs inside the house, and he blames himself, crying: "Attend. Anoint the wound." And the theme is resumed in the third section:

> O we tented our wound all night
> under the homely sheet
>
> and lay as if the cold flat of a blade
> had winded us.
>
> More and more I postulate
> thick healings, like now
>
> as you bend in the shower
> water lives down the tilting stoups of your breasts.

The poem moves painfully from desolation to near consolation. Even in the final section, there are children who "weep out the hot foreign night"; the protagonist's "foul mouth takes it out" on his wife, and they lie "stiff till dawn / attends the pillow." but memory preserves deep within the soft, unmistakable note of love that will save them:

> Yesterday rocks sang when we tapped
> Stalactites in the cave's old, dripping dark—
> Our love calls tiny as a tuning fork.

The slant rhyme brings the sequence to a close; although the baleful atmosphere present from the beginning never quite clears, the lovers seem to have moved closer to affection. One wishes the poem were longer, something that can be wished for very few poems indeed!

A number of poems in the pastoral-folk mode reminiscent of Heaney's earliest work follow "Summer Home." "A Winter's Tale" concerns a mad daughter who likes to prance naked among cattle and bare her breasts to sympathetic neighbors; "Shore Woman" is an energetic monologue full of concrete natural description; and "Maighdean Mara" (Gaelic for mermaid) conjures an eerie scene that is equal to anything else Heaney has written, for it is full of arresting phrases and lines that fit Auden's definition of poetry as "memorable language," as in the first stanza:

> She sleeps now, her cold breasts
> Dandled by undertow,
> Her hair lifted and laid.
> Undulant slow seawrecks
> Cast about skin and thigh,

> Bangles of wort, drifting
> Liens catch, dislodge gently.

One might argue, easily, that the diction here is slightly affected, but I find this side of Heaney attractive. He is a word hoarder, piling his phrases like stones on his bare hill, and his poems are cairns.

The last few poems of *Wintering Out* fan out like the tail of a comet into a less dense language, a looser syntax, a widening of subject matter. "Limbo" and "Bye-child" chill with their stories of mothers who drown or cage their children in henhouses; these are some of the bizarre perversions of love, of "illegitimate spawning." "First Calf" takes up the same theme in the animal kingdom:

> It's a long time since I saw
> The afterbirth on the hedge
> As if the wind smarted
> And streamed bloodshot tears.

So, the "semaphores of hurt / Swaddle and flap on a bush." The compensations of childbirth are celebrated often enough by Heaney, and beautifully, but here there is only confusion and pain. Yet the end note remains one of restoration. "May" is a paeon to Ireland:

> My toecaps sparkle now
> Over the soft fontanel
> Of Ireland.

The poem "Dawn," one of his very best, breathes beginnings, tells of the poet escaping from a scholarly conference, slipping away to the shore, where, he says,

> I got away out by myself
>
> On a scurf of winkles and cockles
> And found myself suddenly
> Unable to move without crunching
> Acres of their crisp delicate turrets.

"Westering" draws the book to a close with characteristic brilliance, entwining in one poem the biographical strand of part 2 with the vision of history witnessed in part 1. The poet sits in California now, pulled up from his native soil like a mandrake, but still "Recalling the last night / In Donegal." Starting out on Good Friday, he saw a "congregation bent / To the studded crucifix." Now, he says,

Under the moon's stigmata

Six thousand miles away,
I imagine untroubled dust,
A loosening gravity,
Christ weighing by his hands.

The pocked moonskin, seen as stigmata, is a luminous emblem, an aegis under which Irish history is enacted, the small and bitter destiny mourned in the book's epigraph, a poem from which the graffito *Is there life before death?* blazes as from a city wall. In a country preoccupied with violence, Christianity seems pagan, and Christ looks more like the tiger than the lamb. To "imagine untroubled dust" is about all a poet can do in these circumstances, and Heaney does it.

North (1975) represents this poet's latest repossession of history, of his tongue, of himself. There is a new directness here, indicated by the title; but Heaney loses none of the suggestive power of controlled ambiguity seen in earlier volumes. His "north" is not just Northern Ireland. The tone of the book rings like a struck anvil; it is stark, cold, brisk as the northerly themes and diction which suffuse these poems. The poet-as-*scop* (Old English minstrel) entertains us with our foibles, with the past (we identify with *his* past) reenacting itself on the native ground. The setting is specifically Irish, of course, but the subject matter obtains for all of us, in any country of the present. His theme, that love is what redeems the past and makes living possible in today's violent world, is set out in the two dedicatory poems, "Sunlight" and "The Seed Cutters," both of which evoke the idyll of remembrance.

Once again, Heaney uses a two-part division, working in the same overall pattern used so efffectively in *Wintering Out.* In the first part, beginning and ending with poems referring to Antaeus, the mythical giant whose strength derived from contact with the ground, Heaney investigates the burden of Irish history once more: the history of possession and repossession of the island by various tribes. The magnificant "Belderg" begins with another of the poet's bog poems. Here, "the soft-piled centuries / Fell open like a glib" to reveal "the stone-age fields, the tomb / Corbelled, turfed and chambered / Floored with dry turf-coomb." This fossilized landscape refers to an Old Norse settlement in County Mayo. The grinding stone of this community, the quern, pulls the tangled feelings of the poet into its vortex:

"But the Norse ring on your tree?"
I passed through the eye of your quern,

> Grist to an ancient mill,
> And in my mind's eye saw
> A world-tree of balanced stones,
> Querns piled like vertebrae,
> The marrow crushed to grounds.

I find these bog poems much more easily comprehensible, but not less dense or complex, than similar poems in *Wintering Out*.

The linguistic exhumation continues, and Heaney uncovers words like *crannog*, an ancient lake; *pampooties*, cowskin sandals; *pash*, head; *obols*, silver coins; and *graip*, a dungfork. The list could be extended for another full page! I will, instead, send the interested reader to the *O.E.D.*, where most of these words can be discovered.

The majestic title poem *North* itself focuses on Viking invasions; in it, the poet returns to a "long strand, / the hammered shod of a bay." Here, the "ocean deafened voices" of the past speak to him, explaining how "Thor's hammer swung / to geography and trade, / thick-witted couplings and revenges." The violence foisted upon man by man is rooted in economic necessity and irrational desires. The "longship's swimming tongue" says, "Lie down / in the word-hoard . . . compose in darkness." This Heaney does, consummately.

He lies down in the word-hoard and whole poems sprout from single word-kernels, such as *ban-hus,* meaning bonehouse:

> I push back
> through dictions,
> Elizabethan canopies,
> Norman devices,
>
> the erotic mayflowers
> of Provence
> and the ivied latins
> of churchmen
>
> to the scop's
> twang, the iron
> flash of consonants
> cleaving the line.

The abrupt, alliterative rhythms, the strong caesurae and kennings, and the eschewal of latinate diction—all contribute to the northern quality of these poems, which occasionally sound like translations from the Old Norse.

Sadism concerns Heaney in "Punishment," another bog poem, but one extending the genre into the political realm. The poet meditates on the execution of some "little adulteress." He says: "I could almost love you / but would have cast, I know, / the stones of silence." He continues:

> I am the artful voyeur
>
> of your brain's exposed
> and darkened combs,
> your muscles' webbing
> and all your numbered bones:
>
> I who have stood dumb
> when your betraying sisters,
> cauled in tar,
> wept by the railings,
>
> who would connive
> in civilized outrage
> yet understand the exact
> and tribal, intimate revenge.

This poem could not be better with its simplicity and fluent movement, its concentration of thought and feeling in a single image, or its wider application to the contemporary Irish situation and, indeed, to the present estate of womanhood. The "stones of silence" theme prefigures the harrowing later poem "Whatever You Say Say Nothing," in which Heaney examines the "famous / Northern reticence, the tight gag of place / And times."

"Strange Fruit" happens to be my favorite among these bog poems, another classic in its way. The archaeological diggers uncover a "girl's head like an exhumed gourd." The following description, dense and physical, is Heaney at his best:

> Oval-faced, prune-skinned, prune-stones for teeth.
> They unswaddled the wet fern of her hair
> And made an exhibition of its coil,
> Let the air at her leathery beauty.

The "Alas, poor Yorick" theme takes on new resonance; for this "murdered, forgotten, nameless, terrible / Beheaded girl" outstares "axe and beautification," outstares "what had begun to feel like reverence." Heaney, in his artful meditation, moves beyond pathos into an eerie objectivity while he still retains compassion. The ancient girl, in her deathless stare, is a poet of sorts, the voyeur of her own demise, the endlessly patient collector of evidence. This is the ideal model for a poet writing of Irish history, the persona of voyeur/accuser.

"Ocean's Love to Ireland" shifts to the Elizabethan colonial possession of Heaney's island, and its theme is summed up in the last line—my principal theme in this essay—"The ground possessed and repossessed." Heaney envisions the English-Irish relation in explicit sexual terms, making literal the metaphor of "possession." "Act of Union," which follows shortly, pursues the analogy further, making the poet's beloved into "the heaving province where our past has grown." He wrings the conceit mercilessly:

> I am the tall kingdom over your shoulder
> That you would neither cajole nor ignore.
> Conquest is a lie. I grow older
> Conceding your half-independent shore
> Within whose borders now my legacy
> Culminates inexorably.

The second half of "Act of Union" concerns itself with fathering, and the inevitable Freudian duel for the possession of the mother:

> His parasitical
> And ignorant little fists already
> Beat at your borders and I know they're cocked
> At me across the water.

A deeply plunging terror underlies this poem, one of Heaney's memorable achievements. The political implications suggest that no treaty will salve the wound inflicted by England on this "ruined maid" of Ireland. To quote William Empson, "It is the pain, it is the pain endures."

Pain, in all its sinister permutations, obsesses Heaney in part 2 of *North*. The ironic "Unacknowledged Legislator's Dream" provides a glimpse of "the troubles," as they are called, from the inside. The poet-persona winds up in jail here: " 'I am honored to add a poet to our list,' " says the commandant in charge:

> In the cell, I wedge myself with outstretched
> arms in the corner and heave, I jump on the concrete
> flags to test them. Were those your eyes just now
> at the hatch?

This reaction, one of mingled fear and detachment, characterizes these political poems; they are poems, I should add, first and must be read *qua* poems, not political tracts. They register one sensitive man's response to an impossible historical situation, a country "where bad news is no longer news." That line occurs in "Whatever You Say Say Nothing," a four-part sequence in a colloquial style harking back to a number of poems in *Death of a Naturalist,* though there is a fresh edge now: "Men die at hand. In blasted street and home / The gelignite's a common sound effect." The pastoral element has disappeared; the pastoral whimsicality of some of the earlier work fades as the poet offers a stinging new version of reality, almost without comment save in the implicit irony of such lines as "Whatever you say, say nothing."

The last sequence of seven poems is called "Singing School," a title summoning the ghost of Yeats; it's theme may be called the growth of the poet, "fostered alike by beauty and by fear." "The Ministry of Fear" begins the sequence; it is a personal history of alienation, starting at school where, Heaney says, "I was so homesick I couldn't eat / the biscuits left to sweeten my exile." The poet feels dispossessed already, uprooted from his country, South Derry, a physical and spiritual exile in his own land. The poem ends with a sinister account of police surrounding Heaney's car when he was out with a girlfriend on a summer night. They jump when he repeats his name: "Seamus?" A sense of the suppressed and evil power represented by the authorities pervades these poems. "A Constable Calls" recollects a time when the R.U.C. (Royal Ulster Constabulary) man came to register the family's crops; the poem displays Heaney's powers of controlled observation and understatement:

> His bicycle stood at the window-sill,
> The rubber cowl of a mud-splasher
> Skirting the front mudguard,
> Its fat black handlegrips
>
> Heating in sunlight, the "spud"
> of the dynamo gleaming and cocked back,
> The pedal treads hanging relieved
> Of the boot of the law.

Heaney's father must account for himself, "making tillage returns / In acres, roods, and perches." We read about "arithmetic and fear," and a boy who "assumed / Small guilts." Relief overwhelms the ending, as the official departs:

> He was snapping the carrier spring
> Over the ledger. His boot pushed off
> And the bicycle ticked, ticked, ticked.

The effect is stunning.

"Orange Drums, Tyrone, 1966" reconstructs the icy spectacle of an Orange parade in stanzas which are harshly "sprung," formal and mimetic of the drums:

> And though the drummers
> Are granted passage through the nodding crowd
> It is the drums preside, like giant tumours.

The poem bites a chunk of reality from the vague air of memory, ending with a vivid line: "The air is pounding like a stethoscope." This ferocity of vision modulates into the gentler meditation "Summer 1969," which finds the poet in Madrid reading a life of Joyce while back in Ulster the violence continues. A natural guilt of escapism wells in the speaker, though he suffers in Spain, too, from the oppressive authorities:

> We talked our way home over starlit plains
> Where patent leather of the Guardia Civil
> Gleamed like fish-bellies in flax-poisoned waters.

The poem ends with a retreat into the cool of the Prado, where Goya's famous "Shootings of the Third of May" presents an analogue to Heaney's role as artist: "He painted with his fists and elbows, flourished / The stained cape of his heart as history charged."

"Fosterage," the penultimate poem of this final sequence, pictures Heaney "with words / Imposing on my tongue like obols" (silver coins). Its grand first line, "Description is revelation," a quotation, could easily serve as an epigraph to Heaney's *oeuvre*. In his poems description gives way, continually, to evaluation, to revelation. The poet becomes seer, "a transparent eyeball" in Emerson's great phrase. He becomes everything and nothing, fixing his eye on the object, transforming it. "Fosterage" ends with a tribute to Hopkins, who sought the *inscape* of each object, who "discerned / The lineaments of patience everywhere." Hopkins, of course, continues as the dominant ancestor for Heaney, the source, the starting point of his own angle of vision. But "Fosterage" remains a preface to poetry, not the thing itself, a prelude to "Exposure," the last poem of "Singing School" and *North* as a whole.

"Exposure" is, again, a meditation of the poet's responsibility in a desperate historical moment. It is a poem about withdrawal, deeply autobiographical; for Heaney has himself in a sense withdrawn into Eire, the south. He lives, now, with his wife, Marie, and children in a stone house in Dublin, looking out to Joyce's fabled Martello tower from *Ulysses*. He is in his own tower of imagining there. "Exposure," being the last poem

in a sequence tracing the growth of a poet, should be truimphal. That it
lacks this note, for the most part, points not to the poet's failure but to a
particular kind of success. Heaney's tower is not Yeats's. His escape is not
into the artifice of eternity but into the recesses of his own solitude; "I walk
through damp leaves," he says,

> Imagining a hero
> On some muddy compound,
> His gift like a slingstone
> Whirled for the desperate.

"How did I end up like this?" he wonders, thinking of "the anvil brains
of some who hate me / As I sit weighing and weighing / My responsible
tristia." A wonderful self-irony permeates "responsible" here as Heaney acknowledges the need for detachment and engagement at the same time.
Yeats could manage this combination, of course; indeed, the cutting edge
of his best poems can be described as the point where these seemingly incompatible realms touch. And Heaney's greatness in "Exposure" derives
from a similar balance of conflicting needs:

> I am neither internee nor informer;
> An inner émigre, grown long-haired
> And thoughtful; a wood-kerne
>
> Escaped from the massacre,
> Taking protective colouring
> From bole and bark, feeling
> Every wind that blows.

Heaney's memorable "wood-kerne" (foot soldier) on the run, blending with
the landscape, feeling every wind that blows (including the wind of guilt),
is an emblem for the modern Irish poet. Without independence and withdrawal, a poet's work becomes infected with the language of propaganda;
but this independence depends, paradoxically, on an intimacy with his environment that has made Heaney Ireland's successor to Yeats.

"Ulster was British," Heaney writes in "Singing School," "but with
no rights on / The English lyric." He claims for himself, now, the rights
denied to his countrymen at an earlier date. He has turned aggressor, re-
possessing the ancient role of *scop,* and his poems have become, progressively, a private *reclamatio*—a protest—and a personal reclamation of a heritage buried under layers of earth and language. Heaney digs with his pen,

exhuming a past which informs and enriches the present and which has designs upon the future. His delving in the philological soil has yielded a poetry of the first order already; indeed, Seamus Heaney is a major poet writing today at the height of his powers.

ANTHONY THWAITE

The Hiding Places of Power

Poets who aren't habituated (by academic circumstance or the lash of earning a living by using their literary wits) to the writing of critical prose may, when they put their hand to it, justify the action in various ways: doing a fellow poet a good turn, showing they can write better than the habitués of Academe or Grub Street, sharing an enthusiasm. This last is the most usual, and has of course a respectable ancestry in T. S. Eliot, who managed to combine careful and rigorous meditations on Middleton, Massinger, Marston, Marvell, etc. with creating the taste by which he himself was and is enjoyed. Philip Larkin, more narrowly and more openly, has done much the same thing with his comments over the years on Hardy and Betjeman. Ted Hughes has, a shade more grandly and cryptically, paid his homage to Shakespeare, Emily Dickinson, Vasko Popa. In all these, enthusiasms have been seen to be both shaping spirits and personal exemplars.

Now Seamus Heaney has collected together some of the prose he has written for various occasions during the years 1968–78. For much of that time, between resigning from a lectureship at Queen's, Belfast, and taking up his present job at a college in Dublin, he was indeed a free lance, living in a cottage in County Wicklow (the setting of many of the poems in *Field Work*), "uncushioned," as he has put it, "by the routine—and salary—of a teaching position." This uncushioned move, Heaney writes in the foreword to *Preoccupations,* was a sign of his determination

> to put the practice of poetry more deliberately at the centre of
> my life. It was a kind of test.

From *The Times Literary Supplement* (October 31, 1980). © 1980 by The Times Literary Supplement.

All that I really knew about the art was derived from whatever poetry I had written, and from those poets who had helped me to write it. I had a half-clarified desire to come to poetic terms with myself by considering the example of others, and to try to bring into focus the little I knew. So when my freelance activities inevitably led to lecturing and reviewing, the focusing began on that occasional basis. But I hope it is clear that the essays selected here are held together by searches for answers to central preoccupying questions: how should a poet properly live and write? What is his relationship to be to his own voice, his own place, his literary heritage and his contemporary world?

The first six pieces in the book, all quite short, form an untitled section on their own though three are headed "Mossbawn" and three "Belfast." They are all, in the best sense, self-centred—informal circumstantial sketches of his upbringing in County Derry, his childhood reading and absorption of "rhymes," his literary apprenticeship as an undergraduate at Queen's (including a handsome tribute to that "agent of change," Philip Hobsbaum, who managed a living transplant of the 1960s "Group" from London to Belfast), and a laconic Christmas 1971 message from the battlefront.

The sixth of these pieces, written in 1972, is really a bridge into the main body of the book: a debate with himself about the "voice," or the two voices of his poetry—"I suppose the feminine element for me involves the matter of Ireland, and the masculine strain is drawn from the involvement with English literature. . . .I began as a poet when my roots were crossed with my reading." All this is expanded and given considerable underpinning in a lecture he gave two years later to the Royal Society of Literature. "Feeling into Words," which takes as its starting point those lines in *The Prelude* where Wordsworth says

> The hiding places of my power
> Seem open; I approach; and then they close;
> I see by glimpses now; when age comes on,
> May scarcely see at all, and I would give,
> While yet we may, as far as words can give,
> A substance and a life to what I feel:
> I would enshrine the spirit of the past
> For future restoration.

"Poetry as revelation of the self to the self" is Heaney's gloss on the process described there by Wordsworth, and also an account of his own processes, which he concentrates into the single metaphor "digging"—the title, in fact, of an early Heaney poem which ("almost proverbial common sense," he says) equates the spade with the pen: the first poem in his first book, *Death of a Naturalist* (1966), and the first poem of his new *Selected Poems*.

One of Heaney's considerable gifts in these prose pieces is that he keeps a proper—and not mock-modest—commonsensical balance, whether he is talking about himself or other poets. He doesn't want to

> overload "Digging" with too much significance. It is a big coarse-grained navvy of a poem, but it is interesting as an example—and not just as an example of what one reviewer called "mud-caked fingers in Russell Square."

Indeed, Clive James's hilarious peat-slabbed lines from the work of "Seamus Feamus" (in *Peregrine Prykke's Pilgrimage*) succeeded because they push the acceptable manner of the original into the unacceptable mannerisms they *might* have become:

> White spoors of cockle plumb
> tight mounds brine-splashed with goat-frost. Futtled, numb.
> I slop the dunt melt of the scurfing bog's
> Black molars to the shred-hung mandrake . . .

The ludicrous denseness cackled at there is a kind of penumbra round certain early Heaney poems: to adapt Yeats on Housman, a mile further and all had been bog.

It was in his third, at the time oddly unsatisfying, book *Wintering Out* (1972) that Heaney began to break away from the bogs, bulls, and buckets that had come to seem a winsomely dandified way of dealing with "the matter of Ireland." His reading of the Danish archaeologist P. V. Glob's *The Bog People* helped the break, and the emblematic power of what he came across there is filled out in some detail in the "Feeling into Words" lecture I mentioned earlier. The bogs, now, were to be turned into something other than topographical features of childhood, accompaniments of other nostalgically recalled days behind the plough and peering down wells—the sort of thing that made me say, on another occasion, that the appeal of Seamus Heaney was something like that of Laurie Lee: not cider with Rosie, exactly, but taties with Paddy, a clear pathway onto urbanized

British O-level syllabuses. The bogs instead became the repository of ancient rituals, ancient cruelties, "in the long rites of Irish political and religious struggles."

Alongside these creative revelations, put to good use by Heaney in such poems as "The Tolland Man" (from *Wintering Out,* and included in these *Selected Poems*), run the excavations and reflections of many of these prose pieces—"the relationship between the almost physiological operations of a poet composing and the music of the finished poem." The refinement and extension of Heaney's art, which reached its striven-for level in *North* (1975), goes hand-in-glove with his strong but delicate handling of other men's flowers. In *Preoccupations,* lectures and reviews show a generosity of spirit, and an acuteness of mind, which can see the best in such different recent poets as Ted Hughes, Geoffrey Hill, Philip Larkin, Theodore Roethke, Hugh MacDiarmid, Stevie Smith, Robert Lowell; among the Irish, Patrick Kavanagh, John Hewitt, John Montague, Paul Muldoon— as well as, presidingly and almost forbiddingly, Yeats; which can find as much nourishment, unobviously, in Wordsworth as in, obviously, Hopkins. In all these plumbings in prose, what is felt for is the nerve of the rhythm, the energy of the word, which, together, reach what Eliot (cited in Heaney's lecture on Hopkins, "The Fire i' the Flint") called "the auditory imagination." This is explained by Heaney as "that feeling for word and syllable reaching down below the ordinary levels of language, uniting the primitive and civilized associations words have accrued."

Although, on the face of it, many of the preoccupations of Heaney's prose may seem to be personal and/or Irish (and perhaps there is no need for the "and/or"), the most impressive single piece in the book is a long lecture called "Englands of the Mind," which takes three poets who "treat England as a region—or rather treat their region as England—in different and complementary ways": Hughes, Hill, and Larkin. Heaney's sensitive and sympathetic discussion of these three concentrates on their speech, their special language, in a way that has eluded most of their explicators and standard bearers, who prefer on the whole to make gestures towards their supposed vatic truths and paraphrasable philosophies. What Heaney establishes is the way in which "their three separate voices are guaranteed by three separate foundations which, when combined, represent almost the total resources of the English language itself," and how these draw on distinct landscapes: Hughes's "northern deposits, the pagan Anglo-Saxon and Norse elements," Hill's "Anglo-Romanesque, touched by the polysyllabic light of Christianity but possessed by darker energies which might be acknowledged as barbaric," and Larkin's broader-based tones, "mannerly but not exquisite, well-bred but not mealy-mouthed," which can range from what Heaney hears as the late-medieval cadences of *Everyman* and Skelton (in Larkin's "Money" and "Self's the Man") to the Cavalier, the late Augustan, the Tennysonian, the Hardyesque, and even the Imagist (in "Going"). This essay is an altogether masterly analysis, precise in its convictions, of a kind that only a poet could achieve and only a specially gifted poet could communicate so effortlessly and scrupulously.

Not that Heaney's mind lacks edges in its genial response in what it confronts. Writing about the *Penguin Book of English Pastoral Verse*, an interesting but highly tendentious anthology, he observes of the editors' approach that "The Marxist broom sweeps the poetic enterprise clean of those somewhat hedonistic impulses towards the satisfactions of aural and formal playout of which poems arise." Granting Hugh MacDiarmid whatever compliments can be granted him, he succinctly characterises what can't. "If Burns and Dunbar are tributaries in the stream of Lallans, the portentous and absurd shadow of William McGonagall sometimes haunts MacDiarmid's English. The epic voice goes epileptic. . . . In attempting a poetry of ideas MacDiarmid can write like a lunatic lexicographer." Heaney can even be reluctantly critical of his admired Robert Lowell (a considerable influence on several of Heaney's most recent poems, not included in the *Selected*) when he looks at *Notebook* and some of its progeny.

Taken together (and taking the unrepresented *Field Work* into account, too), these *Selected Poems* and *Preoccupations* shows Heaney as all of a piece, a man in whom technique and craft (he makes his distinction between them in "Feeling into Words") have made a happy marriage. If he was overpraised for his early poems, as I think he was, he is now in danger of being cut down to size by those repelled by the lumbering tread of the symbolic exegetes and the overattention of the elephantine misreaders. But he seems to me a man who knows his own mind and will not easily be deflected. If, though now "cushioned" again in a teaching job, he chooses to go on dealing in prose with writers whose work engages him, I would like to see him write at length about Shakespeare, about Hardy, about Emily Dickinson, about Louis MacNeice; there is evidence in *Preoccupations* to show the results would be worth reading.

BLAKE MORRISON

The Hedge-School: Field Work

The Muses love me: I shall throw
My gloom and fears to the winds to blow
Over the Cretan seas
Anyhow they please,

Happy to neither know nor care
Which northern king beneath the Bear
From his frost-bitten shore
Threatens the world with war . . .
  —HORACE, *Odes* (trans. James Michie)

Field Work (1979) begins not at the beginning but, as is Heaney's custom, with the last poem of the book that preceded it. "Exposure" is exactly what its title implies—a confessional. Written from the dripping trees of Wicklow (southern, rural, away from the Troubles), it lets us in on its author's worryings over the seemingly incompatible demands of art and social concern. The two previous poems in *North* have shown him receiving conflicting advice about his poetic responsibilities: "try to touch the people," one person urges ("Summer 1969"); "Go your own way. / Do your own work," says another ("Fosterage"). The conflict arises again here as the poet walks through the countryside. On the one hand are those who see poetry as a social instrument, a bludgeoning tool, "a slingtone / Whirled for the desperate." On the other are the friends whose "Beautiful prismatic coun-

---

From *Seamus Heaney.* © 1982 by Blake Morrison. Methuen, 1982.

selling" (a bit "precious" and aesthete-like, the phrase makes them sound)
would have him strive for the "diamond absolutes," the beauty and permanence of the perfectly achieved work of art. These voices sound accusingly
in the poet's head—even the rain seems to "Mutter about let-downs and
erosions"—and an air of wistfulness and defeat hangs over him. But in the
end he rises to an almost manifesto-like self-definition:

> I am neither internee nor informer;
> An inner émigré, grown long-haired
> And thoughtful; a wood-kerne
>
> Escaped from the massacre,
> Taking protective colouring
> From bole and bark, feeling
> Every wind that blows;
>
> Who, blowing up these sparks
> For their meagre heat, have missed
> The once-in-a-lifetime portent,
> The comet's pulsing rose.

Those three semicolons, and the gap between the word "Who" and its an-
tecedent, lend the conclusion of this poem an air of ambiguity; but its drift
is clear. The suggestion is that Heaney, having withdrawn into his art,
"long-haired / And thoughtful," has missed the opportunity to observe a
unique historical moment in the North. But against that we have to consider what missing a "once-in-a-lifetime portent" amounts to when
weighed against the absolutes of art. The poem reaches no tidy resolution,
but for all its tentativeness does seem to move towards a position of
strength: irresolution but independence.

   What "Exposure" leaves us with, *Field Work* takes up and develops.
Its jacket cover reproduces a section of a large-scale map showing the gate-
lodge at Glanmore, County Wicklow, to which Heaney and his family
came to live in July 1972, and where they stayed for four years before making their home in Dublin. The poetry in *Field Work* is deeply conscious of
that move into the Republic and the countryside. Heaney, after all, had
spent his first thirty-three years in the North, nearly half of them in the
city of Belfast, and by 1972 was a public, spokesman-like figure and celeb-
rity there. He also had a teaching job at the Queen's University which he
enjoyed. Although the decision to leave Belfast was on one level practical
and straightforward (he wanted to devote himself full time to writing, and

the offer of the use of a cottage belonging to a Canadian friend, Ann Saddlemeyer, was a chance to break old rhythms and routines), it had many reverberations. He himself described it as "emblematic" and as having a "political dimension," and certainly the press saw it in this way: one Eire newspaper ran the headline "ULSTER POET MOVES SOUTH," while in Belfast *The Protestant Telegraph* devoted a half-page to the move, identifying Heaney as "the well-known Papish propagandist." In such circumstances it was not surprising that the move should have been seen by some as a betrayal of the Northern Catholic community and should have aroused in Heaney feelings of unease and even guilt.

One important consequence was the new seriousness he brought to his thinking about the writer and his responsibilities. As he put it: "Those four years were an important growth time when I was asking myself questions about the proper function of poets and poetry and learning a new commitment to the art." *Field Work* is indeed Heaney's most questioning book, one that returns many times to the issues raised in "Exposure," and one in which the poet is to be found anxiously consulting friends, relations, sibyls, but above all himself: "Who's sorry for our trouble?," "What will become of us?," "What do we say any more / to conjure the salt of our earth?," "how culpable was he / that last night . . . ?," "How perilous is it to choose / not to love the life we're shown?," "What is my apology for poetry?," "Whose is the life / Most dedicated and exemplary?," and so on. There are no easy answers, but there is a drift towards placing art above all else—the "diamond absolutes" are decisively preferred to the "sling-stone / Whirled for the desperate." Heaney's reviews from the mid-1970s bear this development out, suggesting a reaction against the kind of political pressure he had been under in Belfast and to which *North* had been a response. In a review of 1975 he can be found complaining that "internment and the North have become a spectator sport" [*Poems*], and a 1974 account of Mandelstam's relationship with the Russian government claims: "We live here in critical times ourselves, when the idea of poetry as an art is in danger of being overshadowed by a quest for poetry as a diagram of political attitudes. Some commentators have all the fussy literalism of an official from the ministry of truth."

It is in response to such attitudes that Heaney offers his "field work." Teasingly confronting what he calls the "simple-minded" belief that "poems with rural or archaic images . . . aren't engaging with the modern world," he places at the centre of the collection ten highly wrought sonnets about the experience of living in Glanmore, with its mists and wet hedges, its ploughs and tractors, its cuckoos and corncrakes, its rats and deer, its

rowans and elderberries, and so on. The subtext is Heaney's sense of himself as resembling other famous figures who retreated into the sanctuary of
rural life: Horace, in his "leafy privacy" far from Rome (Ann Saddlemeyer's
loan of the Wicklow gate-lodge is like Maecenas' gift of the Sabine farm);
Virgil, whose *Georgics* gave instructions in agriculture; Sweeney, of the
Irish epic poem, who after the noise of battle was turned into a bird and
roamed the countryside. *Field Work* is conscious of appearing to be a similar
withdrawal: the topography is much more restricted than that of *North* (or-
dnance-survey scale), the timescale drastically diminished (four years rather
than 2000), the tone quietly reverential, the subject matter and poetic line
a return to the first two books. "Now the good life could be to cross a
field / And art a paradigm of earth new from the lathe / Of ploughs," he
writes in the first of these sonnets, knowing full well the taunt he is offering to "the world of illiterates and politicians," [*Preoccupations*]. The second
sonnet, too, self-consciously dramatizes a "turning point" in his career,
bringing visually alive that tired critical phrase:

> Then I landed in the hedge-school of Glanmore
> And from the backs of ditches hoped to raise
> A voice caught back off slug-horn and slow chanter
> That might continue, hold, dispel, appease:
> Vowels ploughed into other, opened ground,
> Each verse returning like the plough turned round.

There is a certain amount of twinkling-eyed irony in that first line. For
hedge-schools, as Heaney's friend Brian Friel reminds us in his play *Translations* (1980), were the schools operated by and for Irish Catholic peasants
at a time when no official provision for their education existed. Based in
barns, cowsheds and even the open air, hedge-schools survived until the
introduction of state education in 1831, and were the reason why some
Irish peasants had such a remarkable knowledge of the classics. The Glanmore hedge-school is not, then, to be confused with the Georgian nature-
school: Heaney's pun on the word implies that he has been getting for himself a grass-roots education—"radical" in the original sense of that word.
Field Work is not, in other words, quite the regression it plays at being:
the search for a voice that "might continue, hold, dispel, appease" has not
been abandoned but rather shifted to new ground.

   One feature of this shift is the emphasis now placed on the notion of
"trust": trust between poet and reader, poet and subject matter, but above
all between poet and language. Christopher Ricks rightly makes much of
the trust in *Field Work*, suggesting that the book "could have been created

only by an experienced poet secure in the grounded trust that he is trusted. Heaney is the most trusted poet of our islands." "Trust," however, is a word that Heaney had not used since his "Honeymoon Flight" in *Death of a Naturalist,* which compared the descent of an aircraft to the beginning of a marriage: "Travellers, at this point, can only trust." That trust in trust now returns—or tries to—with the opening poem of *Field Work,* "Oysters," where the travelers are the poet and some companions who have driven to the coast and are "toasting friendship" with a meal of oysters. The oysters have the sense of an emblem, stirring as so often before the poet's historical and political conscience. "Split," "violated," "ripped and shucked and scattered," they threaten to become another of his symbols of ancient barbarism. A harmless platter of them acquires all the harm of an imperialist plunder:

> Over the Alps, packed deep in hay and snow,
> The Romans hauled their oysters south to Rome:
> I saw damp panniers disgorge
> The frond-lipped, brine-stung
> Glut of privilege
>
> And was angry that my trust could not repose
> In the clear light, like poetry or freedom
> Leaning in from sea. I ate the day
> Deliberately, that its tang
> Might quicken me all into verb, pure verb.

The final stanza breaks not just with the four that precede it but with the hardened customs of several years. History, as so often before, unloads its foul lumber, blundering in on the pleasures of the meal and the text: how is the poet to gorge himself when the past disgorges all this? But now, as never before, Heaney is angry with himself for allowing the intrusion. He aspires to a poetry of "clear light," untrammelled by the darkness and opacity of the past. To eat the day is to give oneself up to the present; being "verb, pure verb," liberated from names and nouns and qualifiers, becomes an image of artistic independence. For while the sentence is a miniature social order, requiring strict and responsible behaviour of its constituents, the "pure verb" (on its own, and unsullied) acts as it chooses. In this opening poem Heaney announces his determination to be determined by history no longer: his mind darting freely wherever it will, he will be leant on only by the poetic imagination.

That the imagination may nevertheless continue to tax him with the

matter of the North and its Troubles, the next group of poems in *Field
Work* makes clear. "After a Killing" (the first of "Triptych") was written
after the murder of the British Ambassador to Ireland, Christopher Ewart-
Biggs, in July 1976. The "march at Newry" in "At the Water's Edge" (the
last of "Triptych") took place in March 1972, in protest against the thirteen killings on Bloody Sunday, 30 January 1972. "The Strand at Lough
Beg" is in memory of Colum McCartney, a cousin of Heaney's shot dead
one night while driving home in County Armagh ("The red lamp swung,
the sudden brakes and stalling / Engine, voices, heads hooded and the
cold-nosed gun"). "A Postcard from North Antrim" is an elegy for Sean
Armstrong, a social worker and friend of Heaney's from his days at Queen's
whose "candid forehead stopped / A point-blank teatime bullet." "Casualty" was written for a man called Louis O'Neill, who frequented the pub
run by Heaney's father-in-law and was blown up the Wednesday after
Bloody Sunday. There is also "The Toome Road," which describes the
poet's early-morning encounter with a convoy of British Army vehicles.
Once again we find him asking a question—though less from bafflement
here than from indignation:

> How long were they approaching down my roads
> As if they owned them? The whole country was sleeping.
> I had rights-of-way, fields, cattle in my keeping,
> Tractors hitched to buckrakes in open sheds,
> Silos, chill gates, wet slates, the greens and reds
> Of outhouse roofs. Whom should I run to tell . . . ?

These lines are perhaps intended to recall Patrick Kavanagh's similarly pro-
prietorial "I am king / Of banks and stones and every blooming thing"
(which Heaney quotes in *Preoccupations*), for Kavanagh, too, well understood Northern sensitivity on the matter of "rights-of-way." That expression, which turns up many times in Heaney's poetry, refers here to no
farmer's feud but to a racial and political confrontation—Heaney speaks in
the tones of a native whose territory has been invaded. The poem ends
defiantly by referring to the "untoppled omphalos": this is both the water
pump described in his memories of "Mossbawn"—"*omphalos, omphalos,
omphalos* . . . its blunt and falling music becomes the music of somebody
pumping water at the pump outside our back door"—and the poet's immu-
table tribal loyalties.

Heaney does not, then, leave Ulster behind him while living in
Wicklow, any more than he left Derry behind him while living in Belfast.
But his tone is now elegiac, concerned not to probe the causes of a nation's

sorrow but to mourn the loss of relatives and friends. There are, in fact, no fewer than six elegies in the book, three to victims of the Troubles and three to fellow artists (Robert Lowell, Francis Ledwidge, Sean O'Riada). In "The Guttural Muse" Heaney writes of "the slimy tench / Once called the 'doctor fish' because his slime / Was said to heal the wounds of fish that touched it." Heaney might still like to be that tench, as he thought he was in *Wintering Out* and *North,* a helper and healer. But he confesses to feeling "like some old pike all badged with sores," and becomes instead an embalmer or anointer, his gifts offered to the dead rather than the living, his task to provide fitting burials rather than to think of means to prevent them. It is as an anointer of his dead cousin that he appears, movingly, in "The Strand at Lough Beg," where we see him kneel like Virgil wiping Dante's face with rushes and dew in *Purgatorio:*

> I dab you clean with moss
> Fine as the drizzle out of a low cloud.
> I lift you under the arms and lay you flat.
> With rushes that shoot green again, I plait
> Green scapulars to wear over your shroud.

In *North* Heaney had resurrected the dead, raising the Bog People out of the past. His one effort to perform similar miracles here—"Get up from your blood on the floor," he orders Sean Armstrong ["A Postcard from North Antrim"]—is poignant in its hope against hope.

The changed role Heaney envisages for himself is most fully explored in "Casualty." This poem considers the implications of one of the most haunting deaths of the Troubles—that of an acquaintance who, defying the curfew imposed by Catholics in mourning for the thirteen men shot dead by British paratroopers on Bloody Sunday, was "blown to bits" while out for his customary evening's drinking: the bomb had been planted by his own people. When, in "Punishment," Heaney had considered similar tribal justice—the putting to death of an adulteress, the tarring and feathering of disloyal Catholic girls—his sympathies were balanced between pity for the victims and understanding of the tribe's "exact" revenge, tipping finally towards the latter. Here there is the same impression of earnest reflection on a difficult moral problem: "How culpable was he," Heaney asks, "That last night when he broke / Our tribe's complicity?" Here, however, the imagery works to exculpate the dead man. A fisherman by day, he "drank like a fish / Nightly, naturally / Swimming towards the lure / Of warm lit-up places." *Naturally:* as the word "connive" swung Heaney one way in "Punishment," so that word "naturally" swings him the opposite

way here, insisting that the man could no more help but be individualistic
than can a fish help being obedient to its own rhythms. A loner by instinct
(we learn of the fisherman's shyness and slyness, his preference of a "discreet
dumb-show" to speech), he has none of the "shoaling" habits that would
have enabled him to conform. Thus far Heaney excuses the man; but in the
last section of the poem he goes further, celebrating his independence as a
paradigm of artistic activity:

> To get out early, haul
> Steadily off the bottom,
> Dispraise the catch, and smile
> As you find a rhythm
> Working you, slow mile by mile,
> Into your proper haunt
> Somewhere, well out, beyond . . .

If we were in danger of missing here Heaney's idea of poetry as being
a kind of "catch" from the bottom of the psyche, the words "working" and
"rhythm" leave us in no doubt of the intended analogy. The thinking is of
a traditional Romantic kind, the poet seen as someone whose pursuit of art
places him above and beyond the demands of the tribe. And the governing
spirits of the poem are not Northern poets like Kavanagh and Montague
but those peremptory Southerners Joyce and Yeats: the Joyce who recog-
nized the need of the artist to fly free of the nets of nationality, language
and religion; and the Yeats whose poem "The Fisherman" was written in
the same two-to-three stress line as "Casualty," looks to the same kind of
"wise and simple man" for moral and poetic instruction, and marks the
same kind of turning away from populist ambitions to a poetry that will
be "maybe as cold / and passionate as the dawn." Heaney's is (as he says in
"Casualty") a "tentative art," shyer and less expostulating, more reluctant
than was the poetry of his predecessors to express contempt for the community as a sow eating its farrow or a "fool-driven land." But he comes notice-
ably closer to rejecting its values here than ever before. He speaks of its
"complicity," the word implying not just confederacy by "partnership in
an evil action" *(OED),* and his image of the funeral for the victims of
Bloody Sunday—

> The common funeral
> Unrolled its swaddling band,
> Lapping, tightening

> Till we were braced and bound
> Like brothers in a ring

—has a sense of constriction and suffocation as well as of communion: "swaddling band," benign sounding when applied to new babies, here suggests the oppressiveness of the *Lumpen-proletariat* ("swad" used to mean "mass" or "clump," and "swaddish" means "loutish"); and "braced" and "bound" are similarly destructive of the perfect commonalty that might have been suggested by the image of the ring. The tribe here begins to seem a threat to independence. Two earlier draft versions of "Casualty" had put the matter more blatantly, one describing the observers of the curfew as "wiser hypocrites," the other ending up:

> Sometimes men obtain
> A power when they betray
> And swim out from the shoal,
> Daring to make free.

Heaney's cancellation of these lines suggests that he is still tugged by old currents of feeling; and it is a mark of his tentative art, his desire to make soundings rather than to be resounding, that the final version ends with his continuing to cast about ("Question me again," he asks the fisherman) rather than with a catch. Nevertheless it is hard to mistake the direction in which the poem is moving, and hard not to believe that in the fisherman's alienation from his people—"he would not be held / At home by his own crowd"—Heaney happened on an emblem for his own move to Glanmore.

The image of the circle used in "Casualty" recurs throughout *Field Work*, acting as the linchpin of an argument about art and social responsibility. On the one hand, the circle symbolizes artistic perfection, such as is to be found in the "Glanmore Sonnets," where every last line completes themes taken up in the first, "each verse returning like the plough turned round," or in "The Harvest Bow," whose "golden loops" provide access from the material world into a spiritual one, "gleaning the unsaid off the palpable." On the other hand, circles symbolize domestic and marital perfection, as we find in the "Field Work" sequence, where there are a number of circular motifs—eyes, coins, rings, moons, sunflowers, vaccination marks. Between these two fulfilling possibilities are less positive ones: circles can symbolize artistic self-enclosure, and poets who pursue artistic perfection to the neglect of their family and tribe are likely to find themselves being wished to hell—as Heaney is, amusingly, in "An Afterwards," where his long-suffering wife is described as wanting to "plunge all poets in the ninth circle" and reprovingly demands of him

> Why could you not have, oftener, in our years
>
> Unclenched, and come down laughing from your room
> And walked the twilight with me and your children . . .?

Artistic endeavour takes its toll, excluding even the poet's intimates from its charmed circle. So, too, those who allow the clenched circles of art to be broken by the clenched fists of politics are equally punishable by damnation. In the excellent "Leavings" this is the fate of that desecrator Thomas Cromwell, who was responsible as Henry VIII's Chief Minister for the dissolution of the monasteries, "the sweet tenor latin / forever banished, / the sumptuous windows / threshed clear"; "Which circle does he tread?" for his sins Heaney wonders, again referring to Dante.

Dante's are the most infernal circles of all, and recur at several points in *Field Work,* which concludes with a translation of cantos 32 and 33 of the *Inferno*. The presence of Dante's circles reflects a new emphasis on moral responsibility, an emphasis quite antithetical to the determinism of *North*. "The way we are living, / timorous or bold, / will have been our life," the "Elegy" to Robert Lowell dauntingly begins: ancestry and environment will not suffice to explain our actions; we exercise free choice and are judged accordingly. Heaney's Catholicism, more a matter of local political alignments in his earlier work, here assumes a sterner, explicitly religious dimension. Voices are raised in judgement and warning—"Unless forgiveness finds its nerve," *"Remember the Giver,"* "the sins / Of Ugolino, who betrayed your forts, / Should never have been visited on his sons." But if Dante's influence is discernible in the tones of *Field Work,* it does not make the book merely bleakly admonitory. Reading *The Divine Comedy,* Heaney has said, "is to go through a refining element, to be steadied and reminded of the possible dimensions of life," and his poems too strive to achieve such steadying reminders—moments of grace that block out the island's "comfortless noises." One such moment comes in "After a Killing," [*Field Work*] where suddenly, miraculously, "the heart lifts" because of the simple, restorative appearance of a girl who arrives like Ceres

> Carrying a basket full of new potatoes,
> Three tight green cabbages, and carrots
> With the tops and mould still fresh on them.

In another poem from this same "Triptych" Heaney describes himself wanting "to bow down, to offer up," and this posture, too, is a characteristic of *Field Work:* as well as the "masculine rectitude of the Ten Command-ments" we have the "feminine" humility of a Marian religion, which gen-uflectingly murmurs its devotion to the things of this world—whether a rowan "like a lipsticked girl" or the "slow diminuendo" of a filling bucket. Naming things, as Patrick Kavanagh once said in his poem about a hospi-tal ward, is a sort of religious ceremony, "the love-act and its pledge"; and Heaney loves to name names, reminding us that to "list" once meant not just to document but to love or desire: "When they said *Carrickfergus* I could hear / the frosty echo of saltminers' picks" ["The Singer's House"]; "Elderberry? It is shires dreaming wine" ["Glanmore Sonnets"]; "Pisa! Pisa, your sounds are like a hiss / Sizzling in our country's grassy language" ["Ugolino"].

This Marian reverence for names and objects underlies the success of the love poems (or more properly marriage poems) in *Field Work,* the first ones in Heaney's *oeuvre* to carry an authenticity of feeling. His previous ef-forts to write to and about his wife had foundered, lapsing into Movement mannerism in *Death of a Naturalist* and high-pitched Plath-like confession-alism in *Wintering Out.* Here he discovers that it is through an obsessive objectifying that he can best be subjective, and through a relentless zoo-morphosizing that he can be most tenderly human. Scarcely womanly at all, the poet's wife appears as an otter, a skunk, a sand-martin's nest, and a piece of low-lying land reclaimed from the sea. Though equations of one's lover with natural phenomena are older than even Burns's red, red rose, Heaney takes great risks in choosing such unromantic analogies and in making so much of humdrum blemishes like "the vaccination mark / stretched on your upper arm" ["Field Work"]. But if his wife is "stained," she is "stained to perfection" (as woodstaining enriches the look of wood), and the poems triumphantly justify their chancy procedures by achieving a blend of sexual passion and domestic affection unique in mod-ern British poetry—not, though, unique in American, Robert Lowell's Liz-zie and Harriet poems having been a useful model for Heaney. In "The Skunk" (a very Lowell-like title and poem) the highly erotic "sootfall of your things at bedtime" (the clothes slip as silkily to the ground as do those of Thomas Wyatt's lover "when her loose gown did from her shoul-ders fall") passes to the maritally routine: "Your head-down, tail-up hunt in a bottom drawer / For the black plunge-line nightdress." That "the" in the last line spells husbandly familiarity, not sensual arousal, but the poem sacrifices neither unity of tone nor strong feeling.

The poet's wife is also an important presence in the "Glanmore Son-nets," the central sequence of *Field Work* (it is placed exactly midway through the book), which draws together the themes of art, love, language, and responsibility to be found elsewhere through the collection. The sequence marks Heaney's return not just to the countryside but to the mainstream of English poetry: having begun in imitation of Ted Hughes and then looked more to his own countrymen, he now takes his place in an English lyric tradition that includes Wyatt at one end and Wordsworth at the other. Both these writers are indeed alluded to. Wyatt's "They flee from me . . .," hinted at in "The Skunk," is explicitly drawn on in the dream related in the last Glanmore sonnet, contributing to the poem's erotic memory of the "covenants of flesh":

> And in that dream I dreamt—how like you this?—
> Our first night years ago in that hotel
> When you came with your deliberate kiss . . . (Heaney)

> She caught me in her arms long and small
> There with all sweetly did me kiss
> And softly said *dear heart, how like you this?* (Wyatt)

Wordsworth appears at the beginning of the sequence, referred to nervously in sonnet 3, where the poet brings up " '. . . Dorothy and William—' She interrupts: / 'You're not going to compare us two . . .?' " and lying behind the image of the poet-as-ploughman in the first two sonnets, as a parallel *Preoccupations* passage on Wordsworth's methods of composition makes clear:

> The continuity of the things was what was important, the onward inward pouring out, up and down the gravel path, the crunch and scuffle of the gravel working like a metre or a metronome under the rhythms of the ongoing chaunt, those 'trances of thought and mountings of the mind' somehow aided by the automatic, monotonous turns and returns of the walk. . . .The poet as ploughman, if you like, and the suggestive etymology of the word 'verse' itself is pertinent in this context. 'Verse' comes from the Latin *versus* which could mean a line of poetry but could also mean the turn that a ploughman made at the head of the field as he finished one furrow and faced back into another [*Poems*].

In sonnet 2 this becomes:

> Sensings, mountings from the hiding places,
> Words entering almost the sense of touch. . . .

Vowels ploughed into other, opened ground,
Each verse returning like the plough turned round.

[*Field Work*]

The poem and the essay make clear the extent to which Heaney shares with
Wordsworth a notion of poetry as the opening up of the "hiding places" of
one's power, as a matter of "sensings" and "mountings." (How characteristic
of Heaney, but how like Wordsworth too, those plural participles are: *sensings, mountings, homecomings, leavings, makings, soundings.*) Throughout the
"Glanmore Sonnets" Heaney takes a Wordsworthian delight in the intimate,
creative relationship between poetry and nature: the evening is "crepuscular
and iambic"; a breeze "is cadences"; raindrops are "lush with omen"; the
poet himself is an "etymologist of roots and graftings." It is this evocation of
harmony between land and language which gives the sequence, which has no
obvious surface unity, an underlying force and direction.

In a review of an anthology of pastoral verse, Heaney admits that he
has acquired the habit of talking "of the countryside where we live in
Wicklow as being pastoral rather than rural, trying to impose notions of a
beautified landscape on the word in order to keep 'rural' for the unself-
conscious face of raggle-taggle farmland." The "Glanmore Sonnets" are
self-consciously pastoral right down to their "classical" bay tree and echoes
of Horace and Virgil. Yet the sequence is not, as pastoral verse nowadays
tends to be accused of being, either simplistic or escapist. Knottily tex-
tured, difficult, lush with omen, it does not merely happen on its pleasures
and harmonies but has to wrest them from fragmentation and disorder. Beyond the images of delicate beauty—small ripples across water and heart,
a "rustling and twig-combing breeze," "fuchsia in a drizzling noon"—lies
the constant risk of intrusion and disillusion: "distant gargling tractors,"
clanking trains, a rat that "sways on the briar like infected fruit." Ringed
round by dangers, the poet and his wife succeed in making small epiphanic
clearings. In sonnet 7, for example, the gales warned of on the midnight
shipping forecast give way next morning to the poet's triumphant witness-
ing and saying aloud of "A haven":

> *L'Etoile, Le Guillemot, La Belle Hélène*
> Nursed their bright names this morning in the bay
> That toiled like mortar. It was marvellous
> And actual, I said out loud, 'A haven,'
> The word deepening, clearing, like the sky
> Elsewhere on Minches, Cromarty, The Faroes.
>
> *(Field Work)*

But we are made to understand that such look-we-have-come-throughs are temporary and precarious: as the epilogue to the "Glanmore Sonnets," "September Song," puts it, "We toe the line / between the tree in leaf and the bare tree." Heaney's characterization of himself and his wife, in the final sonnet, as "Lorenzo and Jessica in a cold climate. / Diarmuid and Grainne waiting to be found" adds to this feeling of vulnerability. Both these couples, the first Shakespearean, the second from Celtic myth, fled their homes in order to be together, living in constant danger of discovery and death. Even the final image of the sequence has its chilly undertow: it is not "rest" which is seen on the couple's "dewy dreaming faces" but "respite," a parenthesis rather than a new chapter, the peace that comes not after but between. Thus, when Heaney writes, in "The Harvest Bow," *"The end of art is peace* / Could be the motto of this frail device," it is the qualification of "frail" and "could" that we notice as much as the italicized affirmation. Peace of one sort or another (his own, his readers', his nation's; psychological, civil, and aesthetic) is what all his poetry works towards; and the "Glanmore Sonnets" and *Field Work* come close to attaining peace. But he is too modest, or not confident enough, to want to press the claim: the hedge-school is also the school of hedging.

In many ways the "Glanmore Sonnets" bring Seamus Heaney's poetic development full circle. It was with the silence of his ancestors that he began and it is a similar silence—"a deep no sound," a "dark hush"—that pervades this sonnet sequence. In the meantime, however, he has resolved the tensions which characterized his early work: the formal, measured voice which he once awkwardly struggled to acquire is here achieved without strain; the troubling dichotomy of the explicit and intuitive in his work disappears; and the forms used are traditional ones that now at last embody his distinctive talent. It would be over-neat to make too much of this progression and return: *Field Work* is only the most recent phase in what one hopes will be a long career. But at the level of poetic language it is a crucial collection. In one of the "Glanmore Sonnets" Heaney refers to "the unsayable lights," implying that there exists a special zone into which language (both his and that of other poets) has been unable to penetrate. But *Field Work* promises that those "lights" may become sayable after all because of Heaney's willingness to trust and treasure language, to cede to its authority, to allow himself to be nourished by its deep structures.

This trusting and treasuring not only makes Heaney a far stronger poet in his later work but has had important consequences for British poetry generally, encouraging a new generation of poets to turn to language

itself as a source for poetry and helping bring about a new imaginative freedom and linguistic daring. I mean by that not that other poets have directly imitated him (though there has been an increased volume of sentimental poems about craftsmen and the joys of the countryside, a
development for which his early poetry must be held partly responsible)
but that he has been the key figure in a movement away from the Movement—he more than anyone has shown that it is possible to preserve the
decencies and civilities of post-1945 British verse while breaking with the
rationalistic mode that hampered it for so long. In this Heaney has had his
final revenge on those who like to present him as an archaic outsider.
Shaped in complex and surprising ways by his culture, he has in turn begun to shape the course of poetry in Britain today.

CARLANDA GREEN

The Feminine Principle
in Seamus Heaney's Poetry

When he speaks of the feminine aspect of his poetry, Seamus Heaney is referring to both language and theme. Linguistically, the feminine element is evident in the richness of vowels, the masculine in the acerbity of consonants. In this essay, however, I am concerned with the feminine principle in Heaney's poetry as a thematic element. For Heaney the feminine is associated with the Irish and the Celtic, the masculine with the English and the Anglo-Saxon. The feminine is the emotional, the mysterious, the inspirational; the masculine is the rational, the realistic, the intellectual. The best poetry, he believes, is achieved by a wedding of the two characteristics. In an essay for *The Guardian,* Heaney says:

> I have always listened for poems, they come sometimes like
> bodies come out of a bog, almost complete, seeming to have
> been laid down a long time ago, surfacing with a touch of mys-
> tery. They certainly involve craft and determination, but chance
> and instinct have a role in the thing too. I think the process is
> a kind of somnambulist encounter between masculine will and
> intelligence and feminine clusters of image and emotion.

My use of the term "wedded" and Heaney's reference to the bog images are particularly appropriate in discussing the feminine principle. As a young child Heaney and a friend stripped naked and bathed in a mossy bog. The event was a seminal experience in Heaney's life, so central that

---

From *Ariel* 14, no. 3 (July 1983). © 1983 by The Board of Governors, The University of Calgary.

he says that he still feels "betrothed" to "watery ground." His descent into the bog became the abiding metaphor of his poetry, and the female principle is inseparable from that metaphor whether he is delving into the depths of the earth, the bog, the womb, or the Celtic unconscious of the Irish people. Ultimately, the feminine principle is that which pulls man toward the sustaining earth and encourages his participation in the domestic and religious rituals which give life continuity.

Long before Heaney read P. V. Glob's *The Bog People* and discovered the specific "feminine cluster of images" which became his mythology, he felt an innate kinship with the boggy earth of his native land. The bogland held "the memory of the landscape" for him. He felt an intense need to incorporate his sense of place with his sense of the poetic, to translate the present by viewing it from the perspective of the past. In speaking of John Montague's poetry, Heaney has said that "the ancient feminine religion of Northern Europe is the lens through which [Montague] looks and the landscape becomes a memory, a piety, a loved mother. The present is suffused with the past." Heaney could well be describing his own work. Glob led him specifically to the cult of Nerthus, the fertility goddess of the bogs who was worshipped by the Germanic people of the Bronze and Iron Ages. Evidence of human sacrifice to the "loved mother" Earth has been found in Northern Europe and in Ireland, hence the actual physical connection between the two areas. For Heaney, however, the connection is less geographical than mystical. The cult of the Earth Mother is the "cultural matrix" out of which Heaney derives order and harmony sufficient to regenerate the blighted land of modern Ireland.

The female principle derives, then, from the Earth Mother herself and from man's pull toward the land and toward woman. It is a principle establishing certain basic qualities associated with the female, whether human or animal, animate or inanimate. For Heaney, the feminine essence may be embodied in a woman, an otter, a cow, or a water pump. Wherever it is found, the feminine principle indicates an otherness about the female, an instinctive difference in the way she perceives life and reacts to it. Her actions are often intuitive; she senses, feels things to a greater degree than man so that the felt experience is a commonplace with her. Because he often cannot understand how she knows what she knows, man, chiefly rational, finds her mysterious and often mistrusts her. Without her, however, he is fragmented and disoriented. In Heaney's poetry, man must learn to trust woman and to rely on her superior understanding of life's creative urge. Through union with woman, man finds rejuvenation, increased sensitivity to life's mysteries and self-completion. Because of the potential fulfillment in such a union, life may become a productive continuum rather than a linear frustration. Consequently, the ring or the circle is associated with both the Earth Mother and the feminine principle.

Throughout Heaney's work, the potential for regeneration and rebirth is associated with the ring, whether it be the golden ring of marriage or the cyclical round of the seasons, the harvest, or birth and death. Significantly, the ring, or more specifically the torc, was the single distinguishing characteristic of the earliest representations of Nerthus. Many of her victims wore neckrings or nooses, suggesting that they were consecrated to the goddess to insure fertility of crops, animals, and man as well. Man's sexual union with or marriage to the goddess is a central aspect of the cult of Nerthus. Out of that nexus come regeneration and creativity. I should emphasize again, however, that the ring image, as well as the images of marriage, sexual union, and the bog appear in Heaney's earliest work, prior to his 1969 reading of Glob. The discovery of Nerthus merely gave order and coherence to his perception of the female principle.

In many of the poems in *Death of a Naturalist,* his first book, Heaney pays homage to that principle. He is, in these poems, the questing, newly indoctrinated initiate into the mysteries of life. In "Poem for Marie," he is the child-man whom union with his wife perfects. She expands the finite limits of his narrow, clumsy world to the "new limits" of the inclusive world of "the golden ring." Thus, he matures into completion. The potentially productive power of such a union is suggested in "Honeymoon Flight" in which the new couple are thrust out of "the sure green world" of youth and innocence into a roiling, chaotic world where the elements are unsettled. The couple are frightened of their voyage into a new life. They must trust their ability to achieve the perfection symbolized by "the golden ring" which binds them.

Door into the Dark establishes the feminine principle as the matrix, the dark fertile womb which brings increase to the earth. "The Rite of Spring" describes the process by which a frozen plunger is freed by fire from a pump: "Cooled, we lifted her hatch, / Her entrance was wet, and she came." The consummation of fire and water, of the masculine plunger and the feminine pump, brings forth the life-renewing spring waters. Similar images are evident in "Mother," a poem about a pregnant woman pumping water for her husband's cows. She is weary of her task and her burden, the baby which she describes as the plunger within her. She is also discouraged over the state of her intimate life with her husband. Looking at a "bed-head" which her husband has used as part of the pasture fence, she notes that "it does not jingle for joy any more." Yet she is the Earth Mother, and she finds joy in the winds that blow her skirts about her thighs and "stuff air down {her} throat."

For the first time, the real Earth Mother appears in the last poem of *Door into the Dark*. By the end of that volume, Heaney had read *The Bog People*, and Nerthus makes her appearance in "Bogland" as the womb of earth, her "wet centre . . . bottomless." Her womb gives forth increase of grain and life, but it also sucks into itself great beasts, trees, and men who feel compelled as Heaney does, to dig "inwards and downwards" to learn its secrets.

The impact of Heaney's discovery of the myth of the bog goddess is increasingly evident in his third volume, *Wintering Out,* which has numerous poems concerned with her. "Nerthus" is a brief poem depicting the simple wooden images of the goddess discovered in the bogs. Glob describes a slender branch having a natural fork in it with no markings except the sign of its sex gashed into the wood where the fork begins. The image is headless and armless. Heaney's Nerthus is "an ash fork staked in peat, / Its long grains gathering to the gouged split; / A seasoned, unsleeved taker of the weather."

Further images of the bog goddess appear in "The Tollund Man." The best of Heaney's bog poems, it is about the most famous of Nerthus' victims. The Tollund Man was exhumed in 1950, two thousand years after his consignment to the bogs. He was found in extraordinarily well-preserved form, his face peaceful, his last meal still in his stomach, his throat encircled with the goddess's torc, the sign of his consecration to her. The head of the Tollund Man, all that was preserved of the body, is on display in Aarhus, as Heaney says in his poem. He also describes the cap and girdle worn by the victim as he was cast naked into the bog to join Nerthus, "bridegroom to the goddess." In his emphasis on marriage and rebirth, Heaney captures the sexual and sacred implications of the ritual: "She tightened her torc on him / And opened her fen, / Those dark juices working / Him to a saint's kept body."

The Tollund Man is a good example of Heaney's treatment of the myth. He is not content with exploiting the myth for its sake alone but must relate it to the Irish land which shares topographical and cultural characteristics with the home of the goddess. Thus, the Tollund Man is not an isolated figure from the Iron Age but a saint who might be implored, though he were pagan, to restore the ritual significance of death in contemporary Ireland. In his essay, "Feeling Into Words," Heaney talks about what the Tollund Man and his sacrifice to Nerthus mean to him. He says that there is "an indigenous territorial numen" in Ireland, a feminine numen referred to as Kathleen Ni Houlihan or the poor old woman. Her authority has been usurped by a violent male cult which he identifies with modern violence and historical English violation of Ireland. The sacrificial victims of Nerthus become, for Heaney, "an archetypal pattern" inspiring awe and fear. The fertility ritual of death and consequent rebirth becomes the symbol of a people guided by a feminine sense of place which Heaney believes must be renewed if the present is to be tolerated.

The difference between the present and the past is suggested in "The Last Mummer." Modern man is threatened by physical violence, but in that, he is not unlike ancient man. He is unlike ancient man, however, in that he lacks the sustaining rituals, like that of the mummer, which give life richness and death significance. In contrast to the mummer's celebration of the return of summer, Heaney's modern family celebrates the television set. The "charmed . . . ring" of their gazing faces is a denial of the regenerative cycle symbolized by the mummer at their backs and the mystical significance of "the moon's host elevated in a monstrance of holly trees." The images of the moon, the monstrance and the holly suggest the joyous, fertile principle of the old rites. It is a sacred, female principle which Heaney fears is becoming less intrinsic to the life-styles of his contemporaries.

Though much of the sectarian violence of Ireland fills *Wintering Out,* Heaney perseveres in his faith in the Earth Mother. To establish a new sense of relevance and spiritual coherence in his life, man must return to the ancient mother. He must again join himself to the land, a "woman of old wet leaves," "her breasts an open-work of new straw and harvest bows" ("Land"). In "her loop of silence," he will find his senses awakened and sensitive to the sustaining "soundings" of the past. For modern man, the common earth becomes a bulwark against chaos.

"A Northern Hoard," the longest poem of *Wintering Out,* clearly establishes Heaney's view of the crisis of modern times. Man is uprooted. Having lost his connection with the earth, he is isolated from woman. "The touch of love" is helpless in the encroaching, terrifying war just beyond the "curtained terrace / Where the fault is opening." Faced with losing a sense of the past and the coherence of ancient rituals, the poet searches for the tinder that will "strike a blaze from our dead igneous days." For Heaney, the tinder is that which reaffirms life and hope in the face of the yawning chasm of violence. The strife common to Irish life threatens death and obliteration. Man must turn from violence so that the creative spark may be kindled. Only then will the "moonstruck" body of the Earth Mother thaw and the warmth of "the touch of love" return.

Heaney's concern over rekindling the vital spark in the twentieth-century female counterparts of Nerthus takes particularly modern expression in part 2 of *Wintering Out*. Colin Falck has said that Heaney's later writings lack significant emotion and that he seems unable to deal with "modern areas of the modern world." To the contrary, Heaney is poignantly aware of the difficulty of cultivating faith in marriage and in other rituals in the face of today's anarchic confusion. Beset with so much that is negative, men and women find difficulty in holding on to each other and to the faith that their union is, in fact, the only means to fulfillment. He does not take a simplistic, idealistic view of the modern dilemma whether personal or political.

Heaney returns to the bridal theme in "Wedding Day," a poem which establishes man's dependency on woman because she has the strength to see the ritual of the wedding through to its end in spite of his doubts and her own fears. In this poem, the intrusion of reality into the idealized love of the newlyweds is poignantly depicted in a bit of graffiti on a toilet wall: "a skewered heart / And a legend of love." Man's union with woman is necessary and rewarding, but it is not an easy coexistence. The groom's independence and freedom chafe under female supervision, but eventually, he acknowledges his need for her sustenance. Thus, the new husband seeks comfort at his wife's breast as they leave for the airport.

"Summer Home" is a painful exposé of the couple's ensuing difficulties. The air is fouled by the odour of an insect-infested mat, which can be easily taken out and scalded. The marriage itself cannot be so easily rid of the unpleasant smell of "something in heat / Dogging us, the summer gone sour." The husband blames himself and makes an offering of summer flowers; he is the suppliant to his lady. The flowers and the sex act are the "chrism" to heal and annoint the couple's wounds. Their union, like the ripeness of the summer, is blessed with increase. But children are no magical cure for the difficulties of two people living together. Wounds leave scars and arguments are inevitable. Heaney suggests that only in the fecundity of the "old, dripping dark" of the womb / cave is there hope to find solutions to the difference between them. The cave, like the womb and the wife's breasts, which the poet describes as "stoups" holding the living waters, are images associated with the Earth Mother's regenerative potential.

The bog goddess is explicitly recalled in *North,* Heaney's fourth volume, one in which his concern grows over the contrast between the ritual and ceremony associated with bog worship and the violence and anarchy of his times. In poems such as "Kinship," Heaney reaches downward and inward in order to find a context in which to view modern chaos. "Kinship" is a fine poem which establishes the racial kinship of the Irish with the "hieroglyphic peat" and its secrets of the past. The bog is "the lovenest in the bracken" where Heaney finds the bog goddess, but she appears less attractive than in the earlier poems. Once again, Heaney confronts the complexity of espousing a mythology which condones human sacrifice. As he gets more deeply mired in the politics of Northern Ireland, he sees the victims of the religious strife of his day in an increasingly personal light. He cannot, on one hand, preach the virtues of the bog goddess as the giver of life, without, on the other hand, acknowledging her as the taker of life. In "Kinship," she is "the insatiable bride," both beautiful and terrible. It is necessary to know both aspects of Nerthus if one is to know either. The poet accepts that responsibility, but he refuses to ignore the human, personal tragedy of her insatiable lust.

Because the old balance between life and death has been upset, the victims of the Earth Mother have lost their serenity. So much blood has been spilled on the "mother ground" of Ireland, that it is soured ("Kinship"). The poems of *North* which describe victims of Nerthus reflect a loss of consecration and peacefulness, a condition Heaney relates to the victims of the Irish strife. The face of the "Grauballe Man," for instance, has none of the Tollund Man's peacefulness; it is anguished and strained. Many female sacrificial victims have been beheaded, their golden hair clipped short. In these poems, the poet identifies with the victims; he refuses to become accustomed to the horror of death, for to do so would be to become less than human and no better than those who are untouched by the nameless dead of Ireland.

Despite the grimness of death, Heaney does not give up his faith in the creative aspect of the Earth Mother. He rejects the violence associated with her worship, yet he continues to see potential only in man's union with her. Without woman, man is cut off from the earth; he is lost, as is Ge's son, Antaeus, when he dies at the hand of Hercules. "Hercules and Antaeus" concludes the first part of *North,* and it is significant that there are no poems governed by the female principle in part 2 of that volume. The ring is evident only in such images as the stockade of "machine gun posts" or the Orange drums beating out the rhythms of violence ("Whatever You Say Say Nothing"). The braided torc of the goddess is "the braid cord looped into the revolver butt" of a constable's gun holster ("Singing School"). Circles are evident in the "dark cyclones" of a violent Goya painting, but they imply destruction, not continuity ("Singing School"). These poems reflect Heaney's confrontation of the Irish problem from a political standpoint and less from a mythical one.

In *Field Work,* Heaney returns to the fields and bogs of the Earth Mother and to the significance of myth and ritual in modern times. In this volume, the poet's childhood and the cultural past of his people are the lens through which Heaney looks at the present. "Triptych" illustrates Heaney's quest for rejuvenation. He asks of a young "Sibyl," a youthful Nerthus laden with fruits of the earth, "What will become of us?" She advises him to turn from the worship of the helicoptering cycles of death and violence to the worship of the ancient mysteries. The poet must "go barefoot, foetal and penitential and pray at the water's edge" for the revitalization of his people. Heaney turns from the killing to the living waters which he has always associated with the Earth Mother. Earlier, in "Kinship," he referred to her as the "seedbed, a bag of waters, and a melting grave." Giver and taker of life, she is the source of understanding for the poet and the source of renewal for modern man. The edge of the bog, lake, or stream is holy ground for Heaney. To learn the mysteries of its ancient language, he must revert to a simpler, more innocent posture.

A similar turn back in time is evident in the "Glanmore Sonnets," which depict a ritualistic return to Heaney's youth. The way back is a journey through the darkness of the twilight and dusk. In the light of the risen moon, ancient symbol of the female, the potential restoration of the poet's skill and the quickening of the people are represented in the image of the flight of "a wild white goose / Heard after dark above the drifted house." Out of the "midnight and closedown" comes the possibility of light. The poet is joined with the woman, but she forces him to confront the dreaded rat, long a symbol for Heaney of untold horrors. Once he faces the grim reality of life and passes the ceremonial test of strength and maturity, he is ready for renewal with the moon-faced woman who lies down by his side in a dream reunion of ritualistic love. Thus, the cycle of life is renewed, and peace and hope are once again evident in the "dewy dreaming faces" of the couple.

The four volumes of Heaney's poetry are marked by a strong consciousness of the earthiness of life and the female principle which enunciates it. His discovery of the myth of Nerthus and her symbolic neck ring was a fortuitous event which gave form and substance to the concept of that principle as Heaney saw it in his earliest work. The continuous nature of the life cycle is evident in both the fruition and the death associated with the goddess's cult. For the poet, however, and the times in which he lives, the deathliness of the cycle has become predominant and the balance needs restoring. Important in overcoming the violence and fear of the Irish troubles is faith in the union of male and female. The male must ally himself with the female principle because it is the regenerative, spiritual principle of life. To lose touch with that principle is to lose the cohesion and order of the rituals which sustain life, and thus, to allow the nihilism of war to destroy its potential. Heaney is essentially an optimistic poet, and he draws much of his inspiration from his faith in such rituals and their timeless connection with the female principle.

DOUGLAS DUNN

Heaney Agonistes

A disinterested lyric note can be heard readily enough in Seamus
Heaney's poetry. It is "woodnote," chalumeau, reedy, and Irish. At times
the influence of Ted Hughes is apparent a lyricism as severe and stubborn
as it can be melodious and affectionate, and at pains to be remote from the
elegantly dulcified lilt of English boudoir pastoralism. It is earthy, warm,
sensuous, captivating, but spasmodic, a question of the phrase and short
verse passage. Yet in running through Heaney's poetry visibly enough to
be acknowledged and applauded, it is a feature of his writing and feeling
that has never been fully released. His poetry has been distracted by the
topical and spiritual urgencies that cling to Irish nationality. It seems to
me that it is with that frustrated relationship between lyricism and politics
that *Station Island* deals, and if indirectly, *Sweeney Astray* as well.

Heaney's approach on this internal squabble is fraught with the dangers that attend a poet taking himself seriously in public as opposed to the
privacy of preliminaries and possible changes of tack surfacing in work of
a new or revised kind to be explained after the event. "Away from It All"
remembers the selection of a lobster "the colour of sunk munitions," cook-
ing and eating it. Sated on this enjoyable repast, quotations float into his
head "like rehearsed alibis." This one comes from Czeslaw Milosz's *Native
Realm:*

> I was stretched between contemplation
> of a motionless point
> and the command to participate
> actively in history.

From *London Magazine* 24, no. 8 (November 1984). © 1984 by *London Magazine.*

Connecting with these lines above, the last free-verse stanza of the poem makes it clear that Heaney feels displaced from his "element" by the command to obey history. Like the eaten lobster, he is,

> out of water
> fortified and bewildered.

"Fortified" seems too sure of its defensively ironic status—poetry, or Heaney's poetry, it is implied, is strengthened at the same time as made vulnerable to attack by it's author's participation in history. Indeed, the last phrase as a whole preens itself on being "well chosen." Its conclusiveness looks to me suspiciously like rhetoric. As a summary of what Heaney feels, it is conspicuously neat and inaccurate when compared with the anguished candour of the title sequence, to which "Away from It All" might best be read as a preamble.

Objects are celebrated in his sequence, "Shelf Life," from a chip of granite to a snowshoe. In evoking these talismans, Heaney seems wary and on guard against intrusions on his "contemplation." In "A Stone from Delphi," he refers to himself as a "primitive Hyperborean," a barbarian from Herodotus's travels, and his insignia

> a work-flake from some northern midden
> I could sentimentalise into a shrine.

The off-handedly disgruntled weight of "sentimentalise" is significant. In the past he might have done exactly what he announces as avoiding. It is a small poem, but one among several indications in *Station Island* that Heaney now finds it necessary to revise earlier states of mind.

Rhymes and half-rhymes in "A Migration," as in "Shelf Life," appear naturally arrived at and their unforced effects suggest authority and control at a time when his writing seems shaken into probing after its own inner revaluations. Heaney's ear does not favour a wholehearted accuracy of metre. Instead, he builds up around cadences, often of great beauty. "A Migration" shows a traditional Irish wandering, drawn from a contemporary observation. It is simply told, and the charming, disturbing and perhaps incompetent family of the poem is left to suggest its own importance. Heaney's tact here is admirable, whether as narrative or verse technique.

"Be adept and be dialect," he is told in "Making Strange." A primary theme of *Station Island* might be Heaney's self-proposed return to a simplicity of subject matter and attentiveness to the common lot. Two poems, "An Ulster Twilight" and "The Sandpit" reveal once again his fondness for trade words and the vocabulary of work.

> Carpenter's pencil next, the spoke-shave,
> Fretsaw, auger, rasp and awl,
> A rub with a rag of linseed oil.

These words are far from lost, but in Heaney's verse they look in a state of preservation. He tries to rub them between finger and thumb into poetry. "An Ulster Twilight" also shows Heaney's gift for drawing the quiet moment, Milosz's "motionless point":

> As waterbuckets iced and frost
> Hardened the quiet on roof and post,

which is all the better here for clarity of rhythm, not always Heaney's strong point. Sectarian thoughts creep into the poem, however, when Heaney gives in to an obligation to disclose that the carpenter affectionately recalled as a maker of toys is from a family politically and religiously opposed to his own:

> A doorstep courtesy to shun
> Your father's uniform and gun,
> But, now that I have said it out—
> Maybe none the worse for that.

Even the toymakers of Ulster are not immune.

The sculpted style of "Sheelagh na Gig" comes awkwardly close to self-parody—"hunkered," "pinioned," and the recognitions on which each section ends with an uneasiness that has become predictable. It is a style in danger of petrifaction, and the last line—"a damaged beast with an instrument"—if autobiographically intended, might be corrosively self-important, the result of a concern allowed to run too far into the public domain. Similarly, in "The Loaning," the opening lines risk portentousness and absurdity:

> As I went down the loaning
> the wind shifting in the hedge was like
> an old one's whistling speech. And I knew
> I was in the limbo of lost words.

Telling more than showing is not a characteristic mistake of Heaney's, and the poem goes on to explore successfully a perception of tiny noises, the sound of humanity against the quiet of the earth, the consolations of the "old first place" of one's voice, and the unconsoling truths of knowledge and imagination.

"Station Island," the title sequence, consists of twelve substantial poems. In the first, a reprobate sabbath-breaker calls to him, "Stay clear of all processions!" This is among the best advice a man can hear, and Heaney could have saved himself the trouble of a long sequence if [he] had taken it to heart and gone home. Instead, he continues his pilgrimage on the island and encounters other ghosts from the old and recent past. He meets William Carleton, a folklorist born a Catholic but who converted expediently to the Established Church. His advice is,

> you have to make sense of what comes
> Remember everything and keep your head,
> and avoid treachery

Some meetings are personal, others religious and political. A priest home from the foreign missions with a wasted vocation chastises Heaney for making the pilgrimage at all.

> the god has since withdrawn.
> What are you doing, going through these motions?

He comes across a schoolmaster and a girl from his childhood, and a shopkeeper murdered in the Troubles: " 'Forgive the way I have lived indifferent,' " Heaney says to the man, " 'Forgive my timid circumspect involvement.' " To which the dead man replies: " 'Forgive my eye. All that's above my head.' "

A dead kinsman, an archaeologist, is encountered. " 'You saw that, and you wrote that—not the fact,' " he says,

> You confused evasion and artistic tact.
> The Protestant who shot me through the head
> I accuse directly, but indirectly, you
> who now atone perhaps upon this bed
> for the way you whitewashed ugliness and drew
> the lovely blinds of the *Purgatorio*
> and saccharined my death with morning dew.

Again, this might be taken as a revised attitude to some of the poems in *Field Work*.

In the ninth poem he hears the voice "from blight and hunger" of a dead PIRA man, and then sees the vision of a trumpet from his own boyhood.

> I hate how quick I was to know my place.
> I hate where I was born, hate everything
> That made me biddable and unforthcoming,

Heaney says to himself. These are strong words, shrill feelings to be published even in the nightmarish surrounds of a dream-sequence which is a descent into the moist Hell of Ireland, a lustral walk in search of comfort and renewal.

In the final poem, he meets someone who could be James Joyce, and he advises:

> 'Your obligation
> is not discharged by any common rite.
> What you must do must be done on your own
> so get back in harness. The main thing is to write
> for the joy of it. Cultivate a work-lust
> that imagines its haven like your hands at night
>
> dreaming the sun in the sunspot of a breast.
> You are fasted now, light-headed, dangerous.
> Take off from here. And don't be so earnest.
>
> Let others wear the sackcloth and ashes.
> Let go, let fly, forget.
> You've listened long enough. Now strike your note.'

It is good instruction for the release of poetry. Heaney's dilemma, however, is that the freedoms entailed by it might be bought at a cost of irresponsibility, and that mischief is more difficult to bring off than a loyal or rebellious espousal of political convictions. Whether Heaney can solve this problem and "let go, let fly," remains to be seen, but it is, I submit, unlikely. Forgetting can be as plaquey on the imagination as on the conscience. For Heaney to be free of his qualms and hand-wringings—they are, in poetry, honourable—Ireland would have to be different from what it was and is, England different, and history different. No miracles are likely to be performed on the hideous implacability of these facts.

As a contemporary version of an antique Irish classic, the merits of *Sweeney Astray* seem incontestable—quite simply, the poem is interesting to read. It portrays a harrowing fall from repute and acclaim. Personal despoliation by curse and terror, which is what the poem dramatizes, makes it a bleak work. It should be read with *Station Island* as a measure of the inroads made on Heaney's mind by the times in which he lives. The more

I read it, the more I felt that *Sweeney Astray* imagined more than Sweeney's hapless fall from kingship, the very wilderness into which the imagination travels when the gift of disinterested poetry is lost or corrupted by the obligations that press in on it.

RICHARD ELLMANN

Heaney Agonistes

After the heavily accented melodies of Yeats, and that poet's elegiac celebrations of imaginative glories, Seamus Heaney addresses his readers in a quite different key. He does not overwhelm his subjects; rather he allows them a certain freedom from him, and his sharp conjunctions with them leave their authority and his undiminished. There are none of Yeats's Olympians about; the figures who appear in Heaney's verse have quite human dimensions. Nature for him does not mean the lakes, woods, and swans visible from the big house. Instead, a farmer's son, Heaney sees it as the "dark-clumped grass where cows or horses dunged, / the cluck when pith-lined chestnut-shells split open" (the latter a line that Hopkins would have welcomed). These and much else are things to remember "when you have grown away and stand at last / at the very centre of the empty city." Nature is "sheep's wool on barbed wire," equipment such as a harrow pin, sledge-head, or trowel, as if its center were protrusive objects and not recessive vistas.

Auden complained that Yeats was willing to sacrifice sense to sound. Heaney escapes such an imputation: his sounds are contained, clipped, unlingering, "definite / as a steel nib's downstroke, quick and clean." Even his lyrical passages are tightly reined:

> Windfalls lay at my feet
> those days, clandestine winds
> stirred in our lyric wood:
> restive, quick and silent

From *The New York Review of Books* (March 14, 1985). © 1985 by Richard Ellmann.

> the deer of poetry stood
> in pools of lucent sound
>
> ready to scare,
> as morning and afternoon
> Brigid and her sisters
> came jangling along, down
> the steep hill for water,
> and laboured up again.

Rhymes, when he uses them, are resolutely unemphatic, more obvious effects being shunned. He is fond of assonance, which, as Austin Clarke said, "takes the clapper from the bell of rhyme." Irish poetry since Yeats has been at pains to purge itself of the grand manner, and Heaney austerely excludes it except on state occasions. He likes tough words that sound like dialect, though they are respectably lexical, such as flenge or loaning or slub silk or scutch or Joyce's tundish. Occasional Irish words such as "aisling" (vision) make their appearance. (There were more in previous books.) Compared with Yeats, this contemporary poetry marks its difference by subdued rhythms, less clamant philosophy, less prophetic utterance. "Glimmerings are what the soul's composed of," Heaney declares.

Although unpretentiousness is characteristic of Heaney's verse, the term is not adequate to describe his assured reticences, his unearthing of apt and unexpected images, his proneness to see the visible world as a substance compounded from materials no longer visible but still suspended in it. Behind facts lie myths, not airy ones but myths so durable they seem facts too. In his new collection, his sixth, the opening poem is a brilliant example. It is entitled, ominously, "The Underground." Poet and wife, on their honeymoon, are rushing to a concert in the Albert Hall. She runs ahead, losing buttons from her coat on the way, as he pursues her. On their return to the London underground it is he who leads:

> Honeymooning, moonlighting, late for the Proms,
> Our echoes die in that corridor and now
> I come as Hansel came on the moonlit stones
> Retracing the path back, lifting the buttons
>
> To end up in a draughty lamplit station
> After the trains have gone, the wet track
> Bared and tensed as I am, all attention
> For your step following and damned if I look back.

The bridegroom, not only Hansel but Orpheus (as the bride is not only Gretel but Eurydice) in this new Phlegethon, claims his rights as pursued as well as pursuer.

Heaney has always been fond of myth, of what in "Gifts of Rain" in an earlier book he called self-mockingly "my need for antediluvian love." He feels inside him "a whole late-flooding thaw of ancestors," including the Tolland man and the Grauballe man. Not anthropological ancestors only. A little room is found for godlike presences, of Diana or Venus, of the Irish Niamh and the fertility sprite, the brazen sheelagh na gig. A cornfield becomes the cornfield of Boaz where Ruth labored. Ghosts belong to the congeries of backgrounding selves, and so he praises Hardy, whose grave he visits in one poem, for "the unperturbable ghost life he carried." Looking at a pump in "Changes," Heaney hears its prehistory, "the bite of the spade that sank it," and all that has happened to it since.

At moments this sense of objects as being like people dragging their histories with them moves toward allegory, as in "A Kite for Michael and Christopher," where the soaring kite reminds the poet humorously of the soul, and the sudden feeling of the kite's weight makes him feel "the strumming, rooted, long-tailed pull of grief." He reminds his beloved that their bodies are temples of the Holy Ghost in order to compare the feeling of her underbreast to that of a ciborium in the palm, as if Christianity existed to supply him with erotic imagery. He hunts for precedents for his own feelings, and lights on Milosz's sense of being caught between participating actively in history and contemplating a motionless point, and on Chekhov's recognition of slavery on Sakhalin even as he tries to waken the free man in himself.

The new book has three sections. The lyrics in the first exhibit Heaney's ability to blend recollection with immediate feeling. Wry, spare, compressed, subtle, strange, they have a furtive intensity and excitement. "Poems that explode in silence, / without forcing, without violence," are what he aims at here. He gives only fleeting glimpses of himself, often mocking, as when, in "Sandstone Keepsake," he is "a silhouette not worth bothering about, / out for the evening in scarf and waders," and "from my free state of image and allusion" looks across at watchtowers in Northern Ireland.

The situation in Ulster plays a large part in these poems. Though Heaney apologizes in one for "my timid circumspect involvement," and in another explains, "I have no mettle for the angry role," he cannot for long, as an Ulsterman, take his eyes off the victims on both sides. Yet he acknowledges, as Yeats did, a certain bewilderment, and in one poem,

"Away from It All," resents that with indirection, using a lobster "fortified
and bewildered" as it reaches the boiling pot. In a no-win situation, the
poet's duty is to register compassion, not partisanship.

In the other two sections of his book Heaney offers, as he has not before, two series of connected poems. One of them is based upon *Sweeney
Astray*, his translation published last year of the *Buile Suibhne*. The original
tale, one of the most extraordinary in Irish, dates from the late seventeenth
century, although it has its origins in the seventh. Heaney was attracted to
it, he says, by "the bareness and durability of the writing." The tale is of
Sweeney, an Irish king, who is furious to learn that the priest Ronan is
building a church in his dominions. He confronts Ronan and throws his
psalter in a lake. An otter fishes it out and returns it to Ronan unspotted.
Sweeney continues to dispute until the exasperated priest curses him and
ordains that he be a bird-man, with a bird brain, exiled to the trees. During his subsequent arboreal flitting Sweeney, only as mad as Cassandra,
composes lucid poems. Heaney is less interested in the confrontation of pa-
ganism and Christianity than in Sweeney as the type of the poet, "defying
the constraints of religious, political and domestic obligation," and, more-
over, "displaced, guilty, assuaging himself by his utterance."

The act of translation suggested a kinship of souls as well as of sounds
between Heaney and Sweeney, and he exploits this in his new book. The
series of poems with the general title "Sweeney Redivivus" offers glosses on
the original, somewhere between the point of view of the legendary king
and that of the contemporary poet. Heaney has a lyric earlier in the book
which he calls "Making Strange," and the effect of these new poems is to
take the poet out of the sphere of being in which he usually locates himself
so firmly. He looks at once familiar surroundings, now quite changed,

> and even the range wall of the promenade
> that I press down on for conviction
> hardly tempts me to credit it.

He has "rent the veil of the usual" and is "incredible to myself." He has
to unlearn and learn again from this new perspective of Sweeney among the
starlings. He can even reconsider Ronan's exiling curse and wonder whether
it was not rather that he himself chose to desert the ground and ground-
lings, so "pious and exacting and demeaned." He says of Ronan,

> Give him his due, in the end
>
> he opened my path to a kingdom
> of such scope and neuter allegiance
> my emptiness reigns at its whim.

As in his flight he masters "new rungs of the air," his coffers are "coffers of absence." He delights in his function as "a lookout posted and forgotten." The Sweeney persona enables Heaney to overcome the earth's gravity, to reconsider all things from the vantage point of weightlessness. The solid Heaney world melts a little. At the same time, though no longer "mired in attachment," Sweeney never really leaves the earth behind, and subjects it to sharp and undetached scrutiny, relieved by playfulness.

These poems have their curious effect of stepping backward and forward at once as tanks and steering wheels appear before the twice-born Sweeney's eyes. Good as they are, they are surpassed by the other section, "Station Island," which gives its name to the book. The connected lyrics here represent Heaney's most ambitious work. Station Island, sometimes known as St. Patrick's Purgatory, is an island in Lough Derg, County Donegal, to which for hundreds of years people have made pilgrimages. Among these were two writers, William Carleton and Patrick Kavanagh. In *The Lough Derg Pilgrim* (1829), Carleton described making his way to Lough Derg at the age of nineteen, when he was still an ardent Catholic. (He became a Protestant later.) On the road he catches up with an old woman pilgrim by whom he is eventually fleeced, and Heaney speaks of passing the point where the meeting must have occurred. Carleton concludes with an attack on the "blind, degrading and disgusting idolatry," "the swindling pilgrims, and juggling priests." Kavanagh's poem, written in 1942, also gives an ironic picture, with much attention to the attractions of women pilgrims. Both these predecessors appear to Heaney in the course of the poem, for at Lough Derg, as Yeats says in "The Pilgrim," "All know that all the dead in the world about that place are stuck."

Heaney, no longer a believer, has had the happy thought of making the pilgrimage an all souls' night, with frequent use of Dantean terza rima. The poet encounters a series of familiar ghosts, a woodcutter he has known, an old master from his Anahorish School, a priest friend who died of fever in a mission compound, an athletic schoolfellow killed by the IRA and a second cousin killed by a Protestant, an archaeologist, his mother, a first girlfriend. They tell their stories to this Irish Dante, and tell them well, and implicate him in their replies. But the main burden is carried by Carleton at the beginning, and by Joyce, no Lough Derg pilgrim, at the end. Carleton, whom Heaney respects for "hammering home the shape of things," explains why things must be known and understood:

> "All this is like a trout kept in a spring
> or maggots sown in wounds—
> another life that cleans our element.

> We are earthworms of the earth, and all that
> has gone through us is what will be our trace."

Kavanagh makes a brief appearance, too, rough-hewn and mocking:

> "Sure I might have known
> once I had made the pad, you'd be after me
> sooner or later. Forty-two years on
> and you've got no farther! . . ."
> And then the parting shot. "In my own day
> the odd one came here on the hunt for women."

But Joyce is assigned a role like that of the ghost whom Eliot summons up in *Little Gidding*. The tall man who "seemed blind, though he walked straight as a rush" does not need to be named.

> His voice eddying with the vowels of all rivers
> came back to me, though he did not speak yet,
> a voice like a prosecutor's or a singer's . . .

Joyce completes Heaney's pilgrimage by rejecting it: "Your obligation / is not discharged by any common rite," he tells him. When Heaney raises the question of the Irish using the English language, Joyce is impatient:

> "The English language
> belongs to us. You are raking at dead fires,
>
> a waste of time for somebody your age.
> That subject people stuff is a cod's game,
> infantile, like your peasant pilgrimage.
>
> You lose more of yourself than you redeem
> doing the decent thing. Keep at a tangent.
> When they make the circle wide, it's time to swim
>
> out on your own and fill the element
> with signatures on your own frequency,
> echo soundings, searches, probes, allurements,
>
> elver-gleams in the dark of the whole sea."
> The shower broke in a cloudburst, the tarmac
> fumed and sizzled. As he moved off quickly
>
> the downpour loosed its screens round his straight walk.

Dante paid a loftier tribute when he spoke of Brunetto Latini running off like one racing at Verona and about to win, not lose, the prize. But Heaney's restrained compliment has its force.

The dead poet whom Eliot encountered in *Little Gidding,* also based upon the Dantean passage, is primarily Yeats, who speaks grandly of large matters. In Heaney's poem, Joyce confines himself to the question of the artist's career. There is much to be said for this unportentous vision. It seems fitting that Heaney should find his model not in Yeats, constantly trying to break through the facade of what is, but in Joyce, who "found the living world enough" if sufficiently epiphanized. Joyce's message is a reaffirmation, with the authority of an immortal, of what Heaney has meant in speaking of himself as "an inner émigré" and claiming "a migrant solitude."

Many of these poems have a tough rind as though the author knew that for his purposes deferred comprehension was better than instant. Obliquity suits him. Heaney's talent, a prodigious one, is exfoliating and augmenting here.

HELEN VENDLER

"Echo Soundings, Searches, Probes"

Station Island, also known as St. Patrick's Purgatory, is an island in Lough Derg, in northwest Ireland. It has been a site of pilgrimage for centuries; tradition says that St. Patrick once fasted and prayed there. The island gives its name to Seamus Heaney's purgatorial new collection, containing five years' work—*Station Island* . . . . The book reflects the disquiet of an uprooted life—one of successive dislocations. Heaney's life began in Castledawson, in Northern Ireland; he was educated at St. Columb's College, in Derry, and then at Queen's University, Belfast (where he later taught); he moved in 1972 to the Republic of Ireland, first to Wicklow and later to Dublin, free-lancing and teaching. A stint of teaching at Berkeley, from 1970 to 1971, began his acquaintance with the United States; now he is the Boylston Professor of Rhetoric and Oratory at Harvard, and divides his time between Cambridge and Dublin. Though these dislocations and uprootings have been voluntary, they could not be without effect, and the title poem of the new volume reviews, in a series of memorial encounters, the "stations" of Heaney's life—especially that of his adolescence, hitherto scanted in his work. The poet moves amid a cloud of ghosts, familial, sexual, and professional. Some are admonitory, some reproachful, some encouraging. These spirits appear and disappear after the manner of Dante's purgatorial shades, as the fiction of the poem brings Heaney as one penitent among a crowd of pilgrims to Station Island, where he stays for the obligatory three-day ritual—fasting, sleeping in a dormitory, attending services at the basilica, walking barefoot round the circular stone "beds," or foundations of ruined monastic beehive cells. The difference between Heaney and the other penitents is that he is no longer a

From *The New Yorker* (September 23, 1985). © 1985 by *The New Yorker*.

believer. One of the shades, a young priest, accuses him:

> "What are you doing here?

> All this you were clear of you walked into
> over again. And the god has, as they say, withdrawn.
> What are you doing, going through these motions?
> Unless . . . Unless . . ." Again he was short of breath
> and his whole fevered body yellowed and shook.

> "Unless you are here taking the last look."

"The last look"—traditionally taken before dying—is not quite what Heaney is up to in this sequence, but he certainly uses the twelve "cantos" of the poem to look back at many of his dead: Simon Sweeney, an old "Sabbath-breaker" from Heaney's childhood; the Irish writer William Carleton (1794–1869), who after he became a Protestant wrote *The Lough Derg Pilgrim*, satirizing Catholic superstition; the twentieth-century poet Patrick Kavanagh, who also wrote a poem about the Lough Derg pilgrimage; an invalid relative who died young; the young priest, dead after a few years in the foreign missions; two schoolmasters; the little girl Heaney first felt love for; a college friend shot in his shop by terrorists; an archeologist friend who died young; a cousin murdered by Protestants; an executed Catholic terrorist; a monk who prescribed as penance a translation from John of the Cross; James Joyce. All these characters (with the exception of the invalid young relative) speak to Heaney, and the poem offers a polyphony of admonitions, ranging from the trite ("When you're on the road / give lifts to people, you'll always learn something") to the eloquent—Joyce's advice to the hesitant poet:

> "That subject people stuff is a cod's game,
> infantile, like your peasant pilgrimage.

> You lose more of yourself than you redeem
> doing the decent thing. Keep at a tangent.
> When they make the circle wide, it's time to swim

> out on your own and fill the element
> with signatures on your own frequency,
> echo soundings, searches, probes, allurements,
> elver-gleams in the dark of the whole sea."

More striking than the attributed voices is Heaney's own self-portrait, full of a Chaucerian irony overpainted with Dantesque earnestness. In "Station Island," Heaney is sometimes (as with Joyce) the abashed apprentice, sometimes (as with his murdered cousin) the guilty survivor, sometimes the penitent turning on himself with hallucinatory self-laceration:

> All seemed to run to waste
> As down a swirl of mucky, glittering flood
> Strange polyp floated like a huge corrupt
> Magnolia bloom, surreal as a shed breast
> My softly awash and blanching self-disgust.

Though the narrative armature of "Station Island" is almost staidly conventional—borrowed from Dante, even down to his traditional words for the appearance and fading of ghosts—the writing often moves out, as in the passage I have just quoted, to the limits of description. Heaney has always had extraordinary descriptive powers—dangerous ones; conscious of the rich, lulling seductions of his early verse, he experiments here in resourceful and daring ways with both the maximizing and minimizing of description. The dream passage about the corrupt polyp interrupts lushness with the surgical slash of the shed breast; the same typical self-correction can be seen in a passage where William Carleton plays the surgical role, interrupting the dreamy language of the poet:

> "The alders in the hedge," I said, "mushrooms,
> dark-clumped grass where cows or horses dunged,
> the cluck when pith-lined chestnut shells split open
>
> in your hand, the melt of shells corrupting,
> old jampots in a drain clogged up with mud—"
> But now Carleton was interrupting:
>
> "All this is like a trout kept in a spring
> or maggots sown in wounds—
> another life that cleans our element.
>
> We are earthworms of the earth, and all that
> has gone through us is what will be our trace."
> He turned on his heel when he was saying this
>
> and headed up the road at the same hard pace.

This small sample will do to show why Heaney's lines are not corrupted by pure linguistic revel—as Dylan Thomas's often were, their simpler phonetic indulgence unchecked by astringency. Heaney works, in

Yeats' phrase, to "articulate sweet sounds together" in ways not cloying to
the ear, often restraining his delight in the unforeseen coincidences of language, sometimes allowing the delight to break loose. Under the influence
of Lowell, Heaney pruned his young luxuriance severely in some of the
poems of *Field Work* (1979). The rapturous lyricism of the early poetry,
though never lost, adapted itself to a worldlier tone, released in "Station
Island" into mordant vignettes of Irish social life. Here Heaney describes
the ordination of the young priest and his visits back to the parish from
the missions:

> Blurred oval prints of newly ordained faces,
> "Father" pronounced with a fawning relish,
> the sunlit tears of parents being blessed.
>
> I met a young priest, glossy as a blackbird
>
>   his polished shoes unexpectedly secular beneath
> a pleated, lace-hemmed alb of linen cloth. . . .
>
> "I'm older now than you when you went away,"
>
> I ventured, feeling a strange reversal.
> "I never could see you on the foreign missions.
> I could only see you on a bicycle,
>
> a clerical student home for the summer
> doomed to the decent thing. Visiting neighbours.
> Drinking tea and praising home-made bread.
>
> Something in them would be ratified
> when they saw you at the door in your black suit,
> arriving like some sort of holy mascot."

The village round sketched here would be familiar to anyone raised in Ireland. Heaney's satiric phrases—"fawning relish," "holy mascot"—defamili-
arize the pieties; the sharpness of his eye is matched in such places by
sharpness of tongue. A brave exactness in saying the socially unsayable appears in Heaney's epigrammatic summation of the society of his youth.
Though the nostalgia for his "first kingdom"—so evident in his earliest
poems—is still present, he has added an adult judgment on the deficiencies
of its people:

> They were two-faced and accommodating.
> And seed, breed and generation still

> they are holding on, every bit
> as pious and exacting and demeaned.

The five adjectives and the four nouns in this passage hold on to their places in the lines as if they were sentinels guarding a fort. They cannot be budged (as anyone can discover by trying to put "two-faced" in the place of "demeaned," or "generation" in the place of "seed"). The words act out the tenaciousness of the Catholics of Northern Ireland, surviving in spite of being—necessarily—"two-faced and accommodating." When words fit together in this embedded way, they make a harsh poetry far from the softer verse of Heaney's youth. It is a poetry aiming not at liquidity but at the solidity of the mason's courses.

At the same time, Heaney's native tendernesses, beautifully realized, ornament his pages. In a typical passage, Heaney as a boy sits in a beech tree, where "the very ivy / puzzled its milk-tooth frills and tapers / over the grain." In this short spill of words, there are no obvious beauties of alliteration, assonance, rhyming; instead, there is the pure discovery of language adequate to the combination of ivy and bole. What is the right verb for the way ivy moves over a tree trunk? What is the right word for baby ivy leaves? What are the words for their shape and edges? "Its milk-tooth frills and tapers" becomes the reflexive object of the oddly transitive verb "puzzled" as the ivy instinctively plots out its new route and puts out its young delicate sprays and tendrils at the same time. A poet can find such words only by analogy with his own inner life; he feels what it is like when consciousness or perception leafs itself out along a new puzzling path. When he needs a word for the ivy, it comes from his own kinesthetic awareness of the body. Everywhere, Heaney's inner life gives life to outer life, attaching to it the felt inner coursings of physical and mental existence.

In one *ars poetica,* "The King of the Ditchbacks," Heaney describes this uncertain and tentative effort of the poet to track down his inner stirrings and translate them into words that are at the same time adequate for his perception of the external world. The poet, says Heaney, feels his ghostly other—his phenomenological self, one might say—making a track, an unintelligible code, "a dark morse along the bank;" the poet follows:

> If I stop
> he stops
> like the moon.
>
> He lives in his feet
> and ears, weather-eyed,

all pad and listening,
a denless mover.

A prose poem continues the relationship:

> He was depending on me as I hung out on the limb of a trans-
> lated phrase like a youngster dared out on to an alder branch
> over the whirlpool. . . . I remembered I had been vested for
> this calling.

Like a priest being ordained, Heaney is vested for the calling of poet
in a mysteriously beautiful poem that attempts to exemplify the paradoxical
total naturalness and total social estrangement of the office of the poet. He
recounts the day of his "sense of election," when he was camouflaged and
taken bird hunting:

> When I was taken aside that day
> I had the sense of election:
>
> they dressed my head in a fishnet
> and plaited leafy twigs through meshes
>
> so my vision was a bird's
> at the heart of a thicket
>
> and I spoke as I moved
> like a voice from a shaking bush.

That day, the hunters catch no birds, but Heaney is urged to return in the
fall, "when the gundogs can hardly retrieve / what's brought down." The
poet realizes he will return, but not to hunt; rather, he will return in
spirit, as a watcher, a disguised Keatsian icon of the harvest:

> And I saw myself
> rising to move in that dissimulation,
>
> top-knotted, masked in sheaves, noting
> the fall of birds: a rich young man
>
> leaving everything he had
> for a migrant solitude.

The echo of the Gospel confirms the depth of the election. The elegiac richness of the language argues the aristocracy of the poet's calling, but the
memory of the stealthy self, "a denless mover" living in his senses, argues

also for the intimacy of this aristocracy with the biological origins of all social forms.

The allusion to the Gospel recurs in the last poem of *Station Island*—"On the Road"—where Heaney recalls "that track through corn / where the rich young man / asked his question— / *Master, what must I / do to be saved?*" In raising this ultimate question, Heaney asks what all the self-born must ask: If the gods of the parental hearth, the altars of the local church, the teachers of the native schools do not suffice as guardians and mentors, then where is one to turn? This is the central outcry of Heaney's book, and it leads him first into the affronting encounters with family, school, and church which fill the long title poem. But after that it ushers him into a strange and unpopulated realm, which one can only call the space of writing. The refusal of the social plenum leaves the artist empty, but his kingdom becomes the entire scope of consciousness. The significant word "empty" recurs several times in this volume, notably in "On the Road":

> In my hands
> like a wrested trophy,
> the empty round
> of the steering wheel.

The end of the intellectual, emotional, and aesthetic struggle to discard false gods seems to be a far-stretching emptiness, but it is one in which the steering wheel is in one's own hands, a prize of victory.

"On the Road," seeking a solution to its sense of bewilderment and depletion, drives itself, finally, to a rock wall incised with a prehistoric carving. There it halts, observing the first, ancient human testimony to the power and strength of form—a form that takes its own inspiration from the contours of its rock matrix:

> There a drinking deer
> is cut into rock,
> its haunch and neck
> rise with the contours,
>
> the incised outline
> curves to a strained
> expectant muzzle
> and a nostril flared
>
> at a dried-up source.

The poet would "meditate/that stone-faced vigil" of the drinking deer

until the long dumbfounded
spirit broke cover
to raise a dust
in the font of exhaustion.

"Dumbfounded" is one of the words in this volume (others are "bewildered," "defensive," "evasion," "guilty," "complaisant," and "emptied")
which convey the many confusions and fears undergone by any independent
mind in defining and defending its own solitude. Against these self-
doubts—arising from the social disobedience so necessary for art but so disturbing to the hitherto obedient—are set various phrases of clarity and self-
fortification. Some are sensual—"hands at night / dreaming the sun in the
sunspot of a breast." Others are experiential—"we are earthworms of the
earth, and all that / has gone through us is what will be our trace." Still
others are aesthetic. In his tribute to Hardy, "The Birthplace," for example, Heaney remembers how as a boy he found in Hardy a writer describing
the life he himself was living on an Irish farm. The shock of that first per-
ceived correspondence between life and art closes Heaney's homage:

Everywhere being nowhere,
who can prove
one place more than another?

We come back emptied . . .

Still, was it thirty years ago
I read until first light

for the first time, to finish
The Return of the Native?
The corncrake in the aftergrass

verified himself, and I heard
roosters and dogs, the very same
as if he had written them.

Poems like "The Birthplace" record, as I have said, private moments
of sustenance in the wilderness of middle life. This wilderness necessarily
includes for Heaney the state of his country, and there are many direct, and
some indirect, references here to Heaney's troubled relation to the insoluble
events in Northern Ireland. The dangers of propaganda and of loyalties un-
mediated by intelligence haunt any writer born into historical crisis.
Heaney quotes Czeslaw Milosz's "Native Realm": "I was stretched between

contemplation of a motionless point and the command to participate actively in history." The contemplation of a motionless point—as one pole of the artist's duty—is reflected here in Heaney's ascetic translation, in the "Station Island" sequence, of a poem by John of the Cross on the dark night of the soul; the command to participate actively in history is reflected in the terse and committed poem "Chekhov on Sakhalin," based on a fragment of Chekhov's life. In the poem, Chekhov drains a last glass of Moscow cognac after traveling thousands of miles from Moscow, through Siberia, to the island of Sakhalin, between Russia and Japan; the island is a Russian prison colony, and Chekhov is paying his "debt to medicine" by investigating the penal conditions. He forces himself to watch floggings and then leaves to write about them, "to try for the right tone—not tract, not thesis." Chekhov's predicament is that of any poet trying to write about historical conditions, but the deeper truth of the poem appears in the closing lines, in which Chekhov's own origin ("born, you may say, under the counter") compels him to his present expiatory inquiry, and to a perpetual identification with the convicts:

> He who thought to squeeze
> His slave's blood out and waken the free man
> Shadowed a convict guide through Sakhalin.

For the last twenty years, each of Heaney's books—from *Death of a Naturalist* (1966) through *Station Island*—has exhibited an experimental advance on its predecessors. Without losing his early sensual depth and sympathy, Heaney has added social and political dimensions to his writing. In assimilating the mythical and organic voice of *Door into the Dark* (1969) to the compelled social voice of *Wintering Out* (1972), with its epigraph on "the new camp for the internees," Heaney assumed a civic relation to his larger society—a position consolidated in *North* (1975), one of the few unforgettable single volumes published in English since the modernist era. In *Field Work*, the formality of Heaney's earlier prosody relaxed into a deft and unassuming phrasal and conversational line—a stylistic consequence of letting the political and social dimensions of life in Northern Ireland invade his adolescent world of nests, aeries, and immemorial agricultural rituals. "I remember writing a letter to Brian Friel just after 'North' was published," Heaney once remarked, "saying I no longer wanted a door into the dark—I want a door into the light. . . . I really wanted to come back to be able to use the first person singular to mean me and my lifetime."

It is this completed voice that speaks in *Station Island*. When a poet remakes his voice, everything already said has to be said over, in the new, more adequate tonality and diction. The imagination, as long as it remains alive, never ceases to reconsider and to rewrite the past; its poems are circumscribed by the potential adventures of the voice. If a poetic voice lacks volatility and modulation, it cannot be convincing in dramas of volatility and modulation; if it lacks a public dimension, it cannot enunciate public life; if it is wanting in inwardness, it cannot convey private intensity. To attempt a new complexity of voice is to create future possibilities for one's past; and in this volume Heaney has in effect rescanned his past, using the accomplished and complicated voice of his fifth decade. The earliest voice, the limited one inherited from ancestors, will "have to be unlearned":

> even though from there on everything
> is going to be learning.
>
> So the twine unwinds and loosely widens
> backward through areas that forwarded
> understandings of all I would undertake.

Heaney's present voice benefits from his recent work on *Sweeney Astray* (1984), a translation of a medieval Irish poem, "Buile Suibhne," in which Sweeney, an Irish king, is cursed by the priest Ronan, who turns him into a bird. Sweeney's dour and lively voice from the trees is blended with Heaney's own in the group of poems making up the third part of the *Station Island* volume, a sequence called "Sweeney Redivivus." These poems form a dry and almost peremptory autobiography, stunningly different from the warm-fleshed account given in Heaney's early books.

It is difficult to choose among the Sweeney poems, since they so illuminate each other. For a view of Heaney's current hard poetic, one would have to quote his poem on Cézanne, called simply "An Artist":

> I love the thought of his anger.
> His obstinacy against the rock, his coercion
> of the substance from green apples.
>
> The way he was a dog barking
> at the image of himself barking.
> And his hatred of his own embrace
> of working as the only thing that worked.

For an impression of Sweeney's tart spite—a tone perhaps impossible for Heaney *in propria persona*—one would have to read Sweeney's hatred for the cleric who, bringing Christianity to Ireland, robbed him of his native ground:

If he had stuck to his own
cramp-jawed abbesses and intoners
dibbling round the enclosure,

his Latin and blather of love,
his parchments and scheming
in letters shipped over water—

but no, he overbore
with his unctions and orders,
he had to get in on the ground.

If one wanted to see Heaney's first moments as a modern writer, the old rural life left behind, one would quote "Sweeney Redivivus," the ironically dissolving title poem of the sequence:

Another smell

was blowing off the river, bitter
as night airs in a scutch mill.
The old trees were nowhere,
the hedges thin as penwork
and the whole enclosure lost
under hard paths and sharp-ridged houses.

And there I was, incredible to myself,
among people far too eager to believe me
and my story, even if it happened to be true.

The fine-edged precision of naming in these poems—the line of the hedges thin as penwork, the hard paths and sharp-ridged houses—has become for Heaney the ethic under which he works. He has written more than once about the "cool" temperature of early Irish verse, contrasting it with the warmer and rounder tones of English poetry; his current effort seems to be directed toward retaining the spareness and chill of the early Irish tonality while not forgoing altogether what he has called "those somewhat hedonistic impulses towards the satisfactions of aural and formal play out of which poems arise."

The "aural and formal play" in these poems is satisfyingly subtle. In "The First Gloss," for instance—the four-line poem opening the Sweeney sequence—the formal decisions are very modest: the rhymes are slant; the second couplet is composed of lines shorter than those of the first. But these formal moves stand for the two themes of the poem—disobedience and independence. Heaney imagines in this quatrain the first scribe who decided

to violate a vellum margin with a thought of his own about the sacred word
that he was copying:

> Take hold of the shaft of the pen.
> Subscribe to the first step taken
> from a justified line
> into the margin.

In one of his first poems, "Digging," Heaney had imagined his pen as a
spade, and had made the work of writing poetry strictly analogous, in the
mental sphere, to the physical work of planting and harvesting. This com-
forting fiction has been supplanted in "The First Gloss" by a recognition
of the inherent outlawry and heterodoxy in writing—what it entails in the
way of departure from socially justified limits and from the self-sufficient
sacred word.

Readers who know Heaney's autobiography in verse from previous
books will want to retrace it in this verbally firm and assured but psycho-
logically beset and uncertain mid-life recapitulation. Those interested in
the social history of Ireland can find here Heaney's visceral account of how
things stand, and will notice especially the horrifying record of killings in
the title poem, as well as Sweeney's tragicomic satire on cultural life in
Ireland. (The *mots justes* for personal and public life, past and present, seem
to come to Heaney with the unforced sureness of instinct.) For me, it is
not chiefly the autobiography or the cultural history—though each is accurate with a poet's accuracy—that draws me to this book. Rather, it is a
poetic handling of language so variable that almost any word, image, or
turn of phrase might appear at any moment. In a typical moment, Sweeney
gibes at the monks writing in the scriptorium:

> Under the rumps of lettering
> they herded myopic angers.
> Resentment seeded in the uncurling
> fernheads of their capitals.

Rumps and fernheads, herding and seeding, capitals and angers, resentment and myopia—these words from medicine, ethics, husbandry, botany,
chirography, psychology jostle each other for position. (Of course, there
would be no pleasure in this if the words did not embody as well the metaphorical animus by which Sweeney turns the intellectual scribes into thick-
witted herdsmen, demeans their art to a venomous proliferation.) Heaney's
voice, by turns mythological and journalistic, rural and sophisticated, reminiscent and impatient, stern and yielding, curt and expansive, is one of a

suppleness almost equal to consciousness itself. The two tones he generally avoids—on principle, I imagine, and by temperament—are the prophetic and the denunciatory, those standbys of political poetry. It is arresting to find a poetry so conscious of cultural and social facts which nonetheless remains chiefly a poetry of awareness, observation, and sorrow.

Chronology

1939	Born April 13 in Mossbawn, near Castledawson in County Derry, Northern Ireland, to Roman Catholic parents, as the eldest of their nine children.
1945–51	Attends primary school at Anahorish.
1951–57	Away at boarding school, St. Columb's College, Derry.
1957–61	Attends Queen's University, Belfast, and receives B.A. in English. Writes and publishes poems in university magazines.
1961–62	Postgraduate student at St. Joseph's College of Education in Belfast.
1962–63	Teaches at secondary school in Belfast; publishes poems in newspapers.
1963–66	Lecturer in English at St. Joseph's College; begins to publish poems in prominent English periodicals.
1965	*11 Poems*, a pamphlet, published in Belfast; marries Marie Devlin.
1966	*Death of a Naturalist*; birth of son, Michael.
1966–72	Lecturer in Modern Literature at Queen's University, Belfast.
1968	Birth of son, Christopher.
1969	*Door into the Dark*.
1970–71	Guest Lecturer at University of California, Berkeley.
1972	Moves from Belfast to Ashford in County Wicklow; *Wintering Out*.

1973　　Birth of daughter, Catherine Ann.

1975　　*North.*

1976　　Moves to Dublin.

1977　　Begins still-current appointment as poet-in-residence at Harvard University, one semester per year.

1979　　*Field Work.*

1980　　*Preoccupations: Selected Poems 1968–1978. Poems: 1965–1975.*

1983　　*Sweeney Astray: A Version from the Irish.*

1984　　*Station Island.*

Contributors

HAROLD BLOOM, Sterling Professor of the Humanities at Yale University, is the author of *The Anxiety of Influence*, *Poetry and Repression*, and many other volumes of literary criticism. His forthcoming study, *Freud: Transference and Authority*, attempts a full-scale reading of all of Freud's major writings. A MacArthur Prize Fellow, he is general editor of five series of literary criticism published by Chelsea House.

TERENCE BROWN is the author of *Northern Voices: Poets from Ulster*.

D. E. S. MAXWELL is professor of English at York University, Ontario. He is the author of a study of the Irish writer, Brian Friel.

P. R. KING is the author of *Nine Contemporary Poets*.

ROBERT FITZGERALD was a distinguished poet and translator. He was Boylston Professor of Rhetoric at Harvard University, and the author of *In the Rose of Time*, and *Spring Shade*.

JOHN WILSON FOSTER teaches English at the University of British Columbia.

RITA ZOUTENBIER teaches at the University of Leiden, Amsterdam.

WILLIAM BEDFORD writes frequently on contemporary poetry and is a regular contributor to *Delta*.

JAY PARINI teaches at Middlebury College and has published a study of Theodore Roethke. His volumes of poetry include *Anthracite Country*, and *The Love Run*.

ANTHONY THWAITE is the co-editor of *Encounter*, and a poet and critic. His volumes of poetry include *Home Truths*, *The Owl in the Tree*, and *The Stones of Emptiness*. He is also the author of *Twentieth Century English Poetry*.

BLAKE MORRISON is one of the editors of *The Times Literary Supplement*, and writes extensively on contemporary poetry.

CARLANDA GREEN teaches at the University of Alabama. She is the author of articles on Huxley, Waugh, and Lawrence.

DOUGLAS DUNN is a poet and writer. His poetry includes *The Happier Life*, *Love or Nothing*, and *St. Kilda's Parliament*. He has also edited collections of English poetry, including *A Choice of Byron's Verse*, *Two Decades of Irish Writing*, and *The Poetry of Scotland*.

RICHARD ELLMANN is Woodruff Professor at Emory University. His books include *James Joyce: A Biography*, and *Yeats: The Man and the Masks*.

HELEN VENDLER teaches both at Boston University and at Harvard. Her books include studies of Yeats, Stevens, George Herbert, and Keats.

Bibliography

Alvarez, A. "A Fine Way with Language." *The New York Review of Books*, 6 March, 1980, 16–17.

Bedford, William. "To Set the Darkness Echoing." *Delta* 56 (1977): 2–7.

Bloom, Harold. "The Voice of Kinship." *The Times Literary Supplement*, 8 February, 1980, 137–38.

Breslin, John P. Review of *Station Island*, by Seamus Heaney. *America* 152 (March 1985): 202–3.

Brinton, George. "A Note on Seamus Heaney's *Door into the Dark*." *Contemporary Poetry* 1, no. 2 (1973): 30–34.

Brown, Mary P. "Seamus Heaney and *North*." *Studies* 70 (Winter 1981): 289–98.

Brown, Terence. *Northern Voices: Poets from Ulster*. Dublin: Gill and Macmillan, 1975.

Browne, Joseph. "Violent Prophecies: The Winter and Northern Ireland." *Eire-Ireland* 10 (Summer 1975): 109–99.

Buttel, Robert. *Seamus Heaney*. Lewisburg, Pa.: Bucknell University Press, 1975.

Carson, Ciaran. "Escaped from the Massacre?" *The Honest Ulsterman* 50 (Winter 1975): 183–86.

Curtis, Simon. "Seamus Heaney's *North*." *Critical Quarterly* 18 (Spring 1976): 83–85.

Curtis, Tony, ed. *The Art of Seamus Heaney*. Bridgend, Mid Glamorgan: Poetry Wales Press, 1982.

Donoghue, Denis. Review of *Field Work*, by Seamus Heaney. *The New York Times Book Review*, 2 December, 1979.

Dunn, Douglas. *Two Decades of Irish Writing: A Critical Survey*. Manchester: Carcanet Press, 1975.

———. "Mañana is Now." *Encounter* 45 (November 1975): 76–81.

185

Ehrenpreis, Irvin. "Digging In." *New York Review of Books*, 8 October, 1981, 45–46.

Foster, John Wilson. "The Poetry of Seamus Heaney." *Critical Quarterly* 16, no. 1 (Spring 1974): 35–48.

Gitzen, Julian. "An Irish Imagist." *Studies in the Humanities* 4, no. 2 (1975): 10–13.

Hederman, M. P. "Seamus Heaney: The Reluctant Poet." *Crane Bag* 3, no. 2 (1979): 61–70.

Johnston, Dillan. "The Enabling Ritual: Irish Poetry in the Seventies." *Shenandoah* 25 (Summer 1974): 3–24.

Kiely, Benedict. "A Raid into Dark Corners: The Poems of Seamus Heaney." *The Hollins Critic,* 4 October, 1970: 1–12.

Kinahan, Frank. "Artists on Art: An Interview with Seamus Heaney." *Critical Inquiry* 8 (Spring 1982): 405–14.

Liddy, James. "Ulster Poets and the Catholic Muse." *Eire-Ireland* 13 (Winter 1978): 126–37.

Lloyd, David. "The Two Voices of Seamus Heaney's *North.*" *Ariel* 10 (October 1979): 5–13.

Longley, Edna. "Stars and Horses, Pigs and Trees." *Crane Bag* 3, no. 2 (1979): 54–60.

————. "Heaney: Poet as Critic." *Fortnight* (December 1980): 15–16.

Maxwell, D. E. S. "Imagining the North: Violence and the Writers." *Eire-Ireland* 8 (Summer 1973): 91–107.

McGuiness, Arthur E. " 'Hoarder of the Common Ground': Tradition and Ritual in Seamus Heaney's Poetry." *Eire-Ireland* 13 (Summer 1978): 71–82.

Morrison, Blake. "Out from the School." *New Statesman*, 9 November, 1979, 722–23.

————. "Speech and Reticence: Seamus Heaney's *North.*" In *British Poetry since 1970: A Critical Survey*, edited by Peter Jones and Michael Schmidt, 103–11. Manchester: Carcanet Press, 1980.

————. "Encounters with Familiar Ghosts." Review of *Station Island* and *Sweeney Astray* by Seamus Heaney. *The Times Literary Supplement*, 19 October, 1984, 1191–92.

Murphy, Richard. "Poetry and Terror." *New York Review of Books*, 30 September, 1976, 38–40.

O'Brien, Conor Cruise. "A Slow North-east Wind." *The Listener*, 25 September, 1975, 404–5.

Pinsky, Robert. "Poet and Pilgrim: *Station Island.*" *The New Republic*, 18 February, 1985, 37–39.

Ricks, Christopher. "Lasting Things." *The Listener*, 26 June, 1969, 900–901.

———. "The Mouth, the Meal, the Book." *London Review of Books*, 8 November, 1979, 4–5.

Riddel, Alan. "Poet of Divided Ireland." *Daily Telegraph*, 14 February, 1976, 14.

Schirmer, G. A. "Seamus Heaney: Salvation in Surrender." *Eire-Ireland* 15 (Winter 1980): 139–46.

Sharratt, Bernard. "Memories of the Dying: The Poetry of Seamus Heaney." *New Blackfriars* 57 (July, August 1976): 313–21, 364–77.

Silkin, Jon. "Bedding the Locale." *New Blackfriars* 54 (March 1973): 130–33.

Silverlight, John. "Brooding Images." *The Observer*, 11 November, 1979, 37.

Thwaite, Anthony. "Neighbourly Murders." *The Times Literary Supplement*, 1 August, 1975, 866.

Vendler, Helen. "The Music of What Happens." *The New Yorker*, 28 September, 1981, 146–57.

Waterman, Andrew. "Ulsterectomy." In *Best of the Poetry Year* 6, edited by Dannie Abse, 42–57. London: Robson, 1979.

Acknowledgments

Introduction (originally entitled "The Voice of Kinship") by Harold Bloom from *The Times Literary Supplement* (February 8, 1980), © 1980 by The Times Literary Supplement. Reprinted by permission.

" 'To Set the Darkness Echoing' " by William Bedford from *Delta: A Literary Review* 56 (1977), © 1977 by *Delta*. Reprinted by permission.

"Heaney's Poetic Landscape" by D. E. S. Maxwell from *Two Decades of Irish Writing: A Critical Survey*, edited by Douglas Dunn, © 1975 by D. E. S. Maxwell. Reprinted by permission.

"A Northern Voice" (originally entitled "Four New Voices: Poets of the Present) by Terence Brown, © 1975 by Terence Brown. Reprinted by permission of Gill and Macmillan and Rowman and Littlefield.

"Seamus Heaney: An Appreciation" by Robert Fitzgerald from *The New Republic* (March 27, 1976), © 1976 by The New Republic, Inc. Reprinted by permission.

" 'A Lough Neagh Sequence': Sources and Motifs" (originally entitled "Seamus Heaney's 'A Lough Neagh Sequence': Sources and Motifs") by John Wilson Foster from *Éire-Ireland* 12, no. 2, © 1977 by the Irish American Cultural Institute. Reprinted by permission.

"The Matter of Ireland and the Poetry of Seamus Heaney" by Rita Zoutenbier from *Dutch Quarterly Review* 9, no. 1, © 1979 by the *Dutch Quarterly Review*. Reprinted by permission of Editions Rodopi B. V.

" 'I Step through Origins' " (originally entitled " 'I step through origins' The Poetry of Seamus Heaney") by P. R. King from *Nine Contemporary Poets: A Critical Introduction*, © 1979 by P. R. King. Reprinted by permission of Methuen & Co. Ltd.

"The Ground Possessed" (originally entitled "Seamus Heaney: The Ground Possessed") by Jay Parini from *The Southern Review* 16, no. 1, © 1980 by Jay Parini. Reprinted by permission.

"The Hiding Places of Power" by Anthony Thwaite from *The Times Literary Supplement* (October 31, 1980), © 1980 by The Times Literary Supplement. Reprinted by permission.

"The Hedge-School: *Field Work*" by Blake Morrison from *Seamus Heaney*, © 1982 by Blake Morrison. Reprinted by permission of Methuen.

"The Feminine Principle in Seamus Heaney's Poetry" by Carlanda Green, from *Ariel* 14, no. 3, © 1983 by The Board of Governors, The University of Calgary. Reprinted by permission.

"Heaney Agonistes" by Douglas Dunn from *London Magazine* 24, no. 8, © 1984 by *London Magazine*. Reprinted by permission.

"Heaney Agonistes" by Richard Ellmann from *The New York Review of Books* (March 14, 1985), © 1985 by Richard Ellmann. Reprinted by permission.

" 'Echo Soundings, Searches, Probes' " by Helen Vendler from *The New Yorker* (September 23, 1985), © 1985 by *The New Yorker*. Reprinted by permission.

Index